CONSCIENTIOLOGY

A Brief Introduction to the Science of Consciousness

Cesar Cordioli

CONSCIENTIOLOGY

A Brief Introduction to the Science of Consciousness

Translation: Jaclyn Cowen

EDITARES®

Foz do Iguaçu, Brazil

2022

Conscientiology: A Brief Introduction to the Science of Consciousness

Original title in Portuguese: *Conscienciologia: Breve Introdução à Ciência da Consciência*

The opinions, content, grammar and graphic revisions of this work were made solely by Conscientiology volunteers.

Translation: Jaclyn Cowen
Revision: Jeffrey Lloyd
Proofreading: Jaclyn Cowen and Telma Crespo'
Cover and Layout: Daniel Ronque
Illustration: Rodrigo Clemente and Pedro Marcelino
Typesetting: Epígrafe Editorial

International Cataloging-in-Publication Data

C795c Cordioli, Cesar
Conscientiology : a brief introduction to the science of consciousness / Cesar Cordioli; translated by Jaclyn Cowen; [preface Lilian Zolet and Denise Paro]. – Foz do Iguaçu, PR, Brazil: Editares, 2022.

112 p. ; il.

Book available on print-on-demand

Original title in Portuguese: Consciencioloogia: breve introdução à ciência da consciência

Includes bibliography, Glossary and remissive index

ISBN 978-65-86544-65-7

1. Conscientiology. I. Zolet, Lilian. II. Paro, Denise. III. Title.

CDU 130.122

Beatriz Helena P. de S. Cestari – CRB-10/1708

EDITARES®

Associação Internacional EDITARES
Av. Felipe Wandscheer, no 6.200, sala 100D - Cognópolis
Foz do Iguaçu, PR – Brasil – CEP: 85856-850
Tel/Fax: +55 45 9 9133 2818
Email: editares@editares.org – Website: www.editares.org.br

TABLE OF CONTENTS

FOREWARD

Graphothosenic Interassistantiality

Decoding scientific language in order to universalize it is an exercise of priority interassistantiality and a noble task for those who see the world taking different hues and evolutionary levels into consideration.

With a didactic narrative, this book fulfills the role of conveying introductory concepts of the neoscience conscientiology to the reader, encouraging them to reflect and inquire about classic eschatological questions from philosophy, such as: Who are we? Where do we come from? What did we come to do in this life? Are we just this biological body? Where do we go after we leave this dimension?

The author's merit is to demonstrate the fundamentals of conscientiology and projectiology in a clear way, translating the more complex and nuanced subjects of the evolution of the consciousness into accessible language. By establishing a close dialogue between the text and images, the book innovates by including figures that facilitate understanding key themes related to the consciential paradigm.

In the manner of a talk, the book exposes bioenergetic and parapsychic experiences inherent to all consciousnesses. In each chapter the reader's self-criticism and lucidity about multidimensional and pluriexistential reality is emphasized, thus removing all mystical and dogmatic veils from the subject of parapsychism.

The true core of the evolutionary process is lucid, cosmoethical and interassistantial self-parapsychism. Learning how to effectively apply one's holosomatic skills and abilities is essential for achieving an efficient outcome in one's existential program (proexis).

This work considers such aspects in a comprehensive technical manner, thereby forming the theorical framework of conscientiology for beginners through the task of uncovering multidimensional reality.

This book brilliantly condenses the author's vast years of experience, gathering a collection of facts and parafacts from more than two decades of national and international travels related to conscientiology. There were journeys related to welcoming, orienting and referring innumerous intraphysical and extraphysical consciousnesses, eager for clarification regarding multidimensional self-reality.

The art of transcribing this neoscience's complex concepts to a colloquial and accessible language, without "cheapening" the information, requires a deep understanding of the ideas. We can say that the author squeezed the "mentalsomatic juice" from the neoconstructs acquired through his accumulation of experiences and condensed a small portion of it within this book. In this sense, his undertaking reveals creativity and parapsychic talent.

Unarguably, this book is an example of graphothosenic interassistantiality within the gigantic universe of the science of conscientiology, providing a knowledge-hungry reader with reflections about the consciential neoparadigm while presenting concepts such as multidimensionality, bioenergetics and pluriexistentiality, in which every consciousness is inserted.

Given the claritaskal exemplarism of this book, we can only offer our sincere thanks for the unique opportunity to write these pages in the foreward.

Lilian Zolet and Denise Paro

Cognopolis, Foz do Iguaçu, 11 February, 2018.

INTRODUCTION

Having given free public talks on the sciences of conscientiology, projectiology and its specialties, in many different places, for more than two decades, I felt a responsibility to present in this book the main topics of information provided to thousands of students.

Written in an accessible language, the central purpose of this book is to present introductory concepts of conscientiology through a dialogue, as well as indicate other sources for the reader to further improve their self-knowledge.

To those who are interested, at the end of the book, you will find the bibliographical references used, a list of conscientiology books, and a list of *Conscientiocentric Institutions* (CIs) that research and disseminate these sciences.

The target audience of this publication is one who has recently been in contact with such ideas for the first time and wishes to deepen their study of them.

Imagine yourself in a lecture environment where, little by little, the concepts are shown to you.

I am grateful for the trust placed in me, and I hope your reading of this book will be as pleasant as it was to write.

The Author

1. THE TALK BEGINS...

Hello everyone! Welcome to this book-talk introduction to the science conscientiology and some of its specialties.

We would like to thank you for your willingness to be here gaining new knowledge.

We will have the opportunity to present a couple of initial concepts for you to understand some interesting ideas and, upon finishing, you can ask questions via the contact details provided at the end of this book.

Before starting the talk itself, let's go through some important initial recommendations.

2. INITIAL ADVICE

2.1. PRINCIPLE OF DISBELIEF

The first recommendation, and perhaps one of the most important, which orients all conscientiology studies, is the *principle of disbelief*.

"DON'T BELIEVE IN ANYTHING,

NOT EVEN WHAT YOU ARE TOLD HERE.

EXPERIMENT.

HAVE YOUR OWN EXPERIENCES."

This principle should always be found wherever in the world a conscientiology activity is taking place.

It draws attention to the importance of constantly applying one's critical thinking and never believing *a priori*, in anything anyone says. We should, invariably, submit everything to personal experience. The ideal would be to apply this principle throughout our life, and not just in the context of this conversation.

So, from this moment, it is suggested the reader does not believe *in anything*, including what will be discussed here. Be especially critical, yet seek to be open to new ideas, and always, whenever possible, have your own experiences regarding the topic.

It is also worth remembering that many active volunteers of *Conscientiocentric Institutions* (CIs), which are non-profit civil associations focused on the study of the consciousness and dedicated to the development and dissemination of conscientiology ideas, became volunteers due to this principle of disbelief, as they judge that their free thinking is respected.

Many people are tired of unverifiable absolute truths (dogmas) common to religion or people who consider themselves *owners of the truth*, found in the most varied fields of knowledge. The fact is that such a principle prompts the reader to assume responsibility to not go just on *hearsay*, not to believe in anything, and to submit everything to their critical thinking.

Although seemingly simple, the adoption of this idea is capable of promoting a true positive revolution in the consciousness' entire existence, modifying their way of acting.

A science is constructed through a lot of research, questioning and debate. Without this, it becomes dogmatism. Hence the natural reason for the existence of the *principle of disbelief* leading to healthy consciential evolution.

2.2. NOMENCLATURE

Every science, even by virtue of its findings, needs to develop its own language. Analyze any science and you will see it has specific terminology, that is, *neologisms* to define its ideas.

Sometimes, the need for new words can be due to a debased connotation of a given term. The word was already contaminated by so many meanings that it tends to hinder the preciseness of its intended use.

Two observations are pertinent here:

1. – Remain open to learning new words within the universe of conscientiology and projectiology *(and you will find that they exist in the thousands).* A person who wants to learn something new needs to be willing to learn new words.

2. – Not all concepts presented by conscientiology are 100% new. Some ideas may have already existed in other lines of knowledge for a long time and be known by other names. However, there is great merit in assigning a new term to such ideas, specifically: providing a rational explanation, based on scientific logic, of a series of pieces of information previously scattered or shrouded in a mystical aura, which often made it difficult to clearly understand them.

2.3. OBJECTIVES OF THIS BOOK-TALK

Another important piece of advice is that, in a short talk like this one, it is impossible to thoroughly explore conscientiology, which currently has more than 1000 specialties or corresponding subsciences.

A general explanation is what is intended here or, in other words, a broad *brushstroke* of some initial concepts. Therefore, the objective is not to exhaustively delve into the topics addressed. The aim is to arouse the curiosity of an interested researcher.

Among other topics we will cover the following:

– Conscientiology.

– Conscientiail paradigm.

– Holosoma: soma, energosoma, psychosoma and mentalsoma.

– Chakras: primary and secondary.

– Basic Mobilization of Energies (BME).

– Lucid projection and projective techniques.

– Multidimensionality.

– Existential seriality.

– Some advanced conscientiology topics, such as: existential program (proexis), *Intermissive Course* (IC), thosene, holomaturity, cosmoethics, intraconsciential recycling (recin), personal energetic task (penta), consciential bond, Cognopolis, conscientiology and the Encyclopedia of Conscientiology specialties, will be presented at the end.

So, let's get started...

3. CONSCIENTIOLOGY

3.1. WHAT IS IT FOR?

For as long as the world has existed, there are certain basic questions that challenge humanity to seek answers. Who are we? What did we come here to do in this life? Where will we go when we die? Among numerous others.

Over time, religion, in its various strands, sought to provide answers. It doesn't seem to have done so well, essentially because it ends up generating more dependencies than solutions. Not to mention the manipulation done in the name of temporal power.

While philosophy is extremely useful in some contexts, it often losses itself due to an absence of empirical experience, that is, in practically applying its knowledge. This frequently results in a hermetic discourse difficult to be grasped by common public.

On the other hand, conventional science has not succeeded in answering such questions, limiting itself to coldly observing the object researched, and letting the most important entity, the consciousness, be jettisoned from the study.

It is in this context that *conscientiology* arises, with a proposal to scientifically investigate consciousness in its various forms and facets.

In essence, this new branch of science aims to increase *self-knowledge*. Conscientiology provides conditions for a person to live better with themselves, to be happier, or in other words to provide *self-assistance*, which will generate repercussions in every sphere of activity in one's life. Consequently, this increases the level of *interassistantiality* in favor of oneself and other consciousnesses.

3.2. WHAT IS IT?

Conscientiology is a new science that, as its name implies, primarily aims to study the consciousness (*logos* = study; *conscientia* = consciousness) and everything related to it.

We can understand a consciousness as being the *self*, *ego*, *I*, the *essence* of a person, thus, who you really are.

Another way of defining conscientiology is by its opposite, that is, what it *is not*. For example: it *is not* a sect, nor a religion, nor gurulatry, nor a temple of ascended masters. Also it *is not* Scientology (a religion founded in California, in the 1950s by L. Ron Hubbard, a writer of science fiction books), despite some similarity in the name.

Conscientiology is a science that shows the need for a consciousness to be responsible for the direction of their evolution. As such, it goes against the *status quo* of fossilizing mysticisms that have existed for thousands of years on this planet, and are often only aimed at exploiting or enriching many other consciousnesses.

The science arose in 1979 in Brazil through physician Waldo Vieira (1932 – 2015), who coined the term in his book *Projections of the Consciousness: A Diary of Out of Body Experiences*. Its foundations were laid in 1994 with the treatise *700 Conscientiology Experiments*, by the same author, and rapidly expanded to hundreds of cities within Brazil and around the world.

Everything we study in the universe has some relationship with the consciousness, even if indirect and unsuspected. In some way, everything has a relationship with you and, therefore, with conscientiology. From this we can see how wide the field of study of this science is.

It is important research, as it has a larger goal, namely, the *evolution of consciousness*. Every effort of conscientiology is in order to provide the means to promote this change.

Conscientiology seeks to study and provide theories for every phenomena linked to human nature, including those often considered fanciful, paranormal etc., and provide logical and rational explanations for them.

4. CONSCIENTIAL PARADIGM

What makes conscientiology different from traditional science is the model used for its research: the *consciential paradigm*. This considers the existence of a being's different vehicles of manifestation, multiple existences and dimensions, thus transcending the physical universe.

What differentiates, for example, conscientiology from psychology, another science that also studies the consciousness, is the paradigm used.

Every science presents a model on which its hypotheses and theories are based. It is like, by way of a simple analogy, the *glasses* through which one sees the surrounding universe.

If the lens are blue, the reader will see a blue world. If it is blurry, they will have difficulty seeing. If scratched, they will be points where vision is impaired. And so on.

In this case, the paradigm used by conscientiology is, as one would expect from the name, *consciential*, that is, it puts the integral consciousness at the center of its focus.

This means that research is conducted in a *conscientiocentric* manner, with the practical objective of improving the peoples' lives, by increasing self-knowledge and knowledge about the universe in which we are all inserted.

By understanding the consciential paradigm, you will be able to understand the foundations of conscientiology.

Three pillars stand out, from among many: the *holosoma*, *multidimensionality* and *existential seriality*, which we will now take a look at.

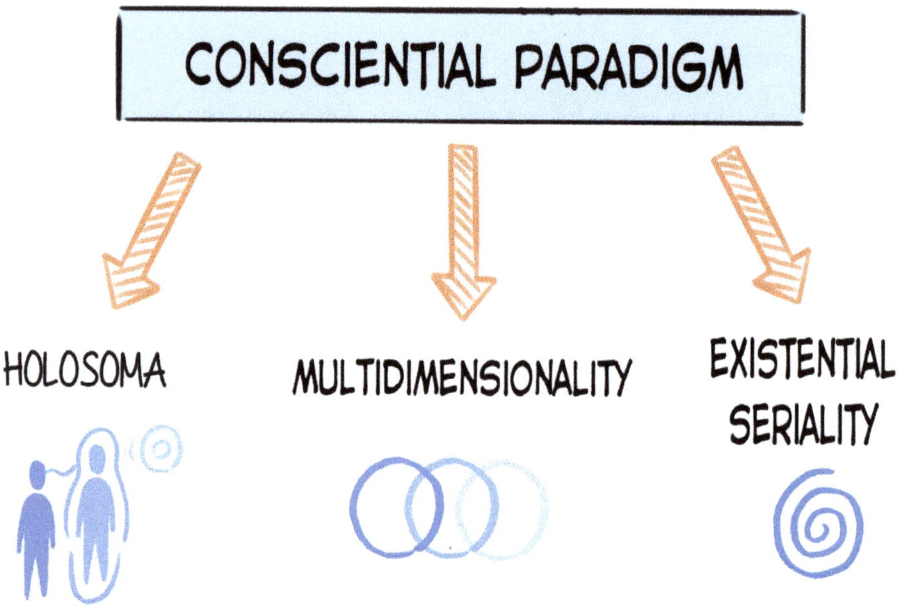

Figure 1. Consciential Paradigm.

4.1. HOLOSOMA

From the perspective of conscientiology, you *are not* only the physical body. You are an eternal consciousness who manifests through a set of bodies, called the *holosoma* (*holo* = entire, set, whole; *soma* = body)

According to this science, there are 4 basic bodies or *vehicles of manifestation of the consciousness* (VMCs). They are:

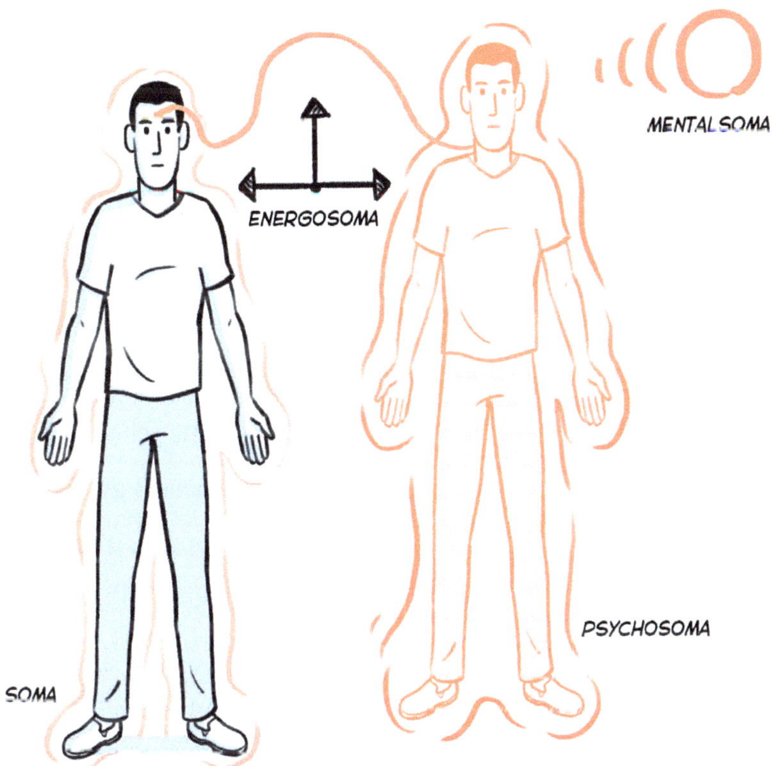

Figure 2. Holosoma.

– **Soma:** nothing new here, it is also known as the physical body, and is the rustic tip of the holosoma. It is the densest vehicle and belongs to the common experience of human existence.

– **Energosoma:** is the consciousness' body of energies, also known as the holochakra (*holo* = set, whole; *chakra* = fulcrum or vortex of energy), energetic double, etheric double among numerous other names. It is in fact a very dynamic body, with direct intervehicular relationships with other vehicles, as we will see later. If we were to again use an analogy, in the form of a sandwich, we could say that the soma is one slice of bread and the psychosoma (see below) is another, with the energosoma in the middle, acting like the filling or that which binds them together.

– **Psychosoma:** also called the astral body, perispirit, or body of emotions, among other denominations. It is the body that habitually maintains a humanoid form, has a number of characteristics such as a tremendous ease in shaping itself (plasticity), and a strong influence on emotions. It continues to be considered the *biological organizing model* (BOM), that is, it is understood that the soma is structured from it. This is the vehicle through which the ordinary, most common, out-of-body experiences are realized. These experiences are commonly called astral projections, among other names, and are more technically known as lucid projections (LP), which we will later study in more detail.

– **Mentalsoma:** known as the mental body or body of ideas, among other names, strictly speaking it is considered to be the seat of the consciousness. In conscientiology, it is considered the most advanced vehicle of manifestation known of, at our current evolutionary stage. Due to its very evolved nature our fuller understanding of it remains somewhat obscured.

– These are the 4 *vehicles of manifestation of the consciousness* (VMCs), or bodies, that we will look at in more detail below.

4.1.1. SOMA

Despite this being the most common body, that is, the physical body of our human existence that everyone has and recognizes, it acquires special importance within conscientiology. Due to it we can manifest in the intraphysical dimension, evolve, expand our self-knowledge, help others, reconcile with past adversaries, and fulfill the existential program (which will be covered in a later chapter), among many other functions.

It is therefore up to each of us to take good care of our soma (given there is no spare), in order to enable productive longevity and make the most of each life, in favor of consciential evolution.

Caring for the soma includes: a balanced diet, an adequate amount of sleep, physical exercise, regular health check-ups, practicing healthy sexuality, and rest, among numerous other actions.

It is worth remembering that everything contributing to the proper maintenance of the soma will also have repercussions on the other vehicles of manifestation, resulting in more balanced energies, feelings and thoughts.

4.1.2. ENERGOSOMA

4.1.2.1. CHAKRAS

It is in the energosoma that we find the famous chakras, the energy points that make up the bioenergetic body. Our vehicle of energies contains thousands of these points.

They are employed, for example, in the practice of acupuncture, moxibustion, acupressure, among many other techniques.

Some of these points stand out because of their importance and are considered the main or primary chakras. In addition there are a great number of secondary chakras, of which we will highlight three. They are:

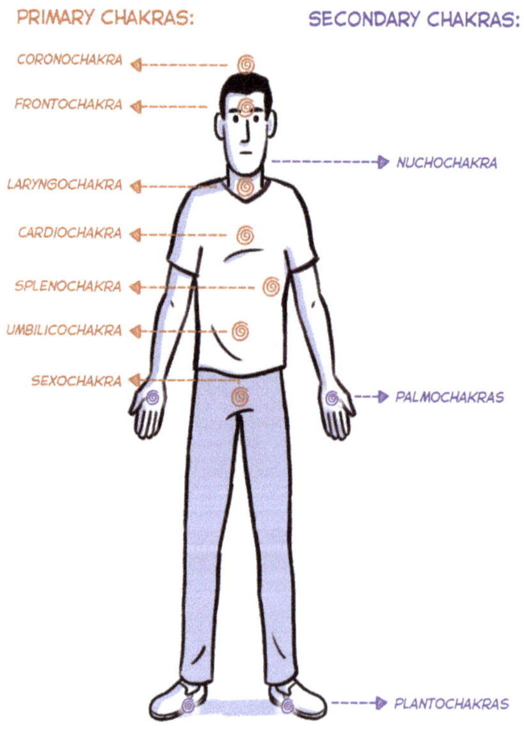

Figure 3. Energosoma.

Sexochakra: located in the perineum region, facing downwards. As the name implies it is closely related to the sexuality and basic energy of the consciousness.

Umbilicochakra: located slightly below the navel region. It is related to the soma's digestive activities and solar plexus.

Splenochakra: located in the spleen region, this energy point is closely related to the equilibrating of energies in the other chakras.

Cardiochakra: located in the heart region, slightly left of center in the chest. As the name suggests, it is directly related to cardiac activities and emotions. A common example is a consciousness with emotional problems who say they feel "tightness in the chest".

Laryngochakra: located in the larynx region, it is closely connected with the consciousness' speech and communicative processes, beyond the cardiochakra. Thus, it is common for a person who is emotional to experience impeded speech.

Frontochakra: located in the center of the forehead or brow. Very famous in occult circles, and also known as the third sight or third eye. It is directly related to the phenomenon of *clairvoyance* (seeing beyond the physical dimension) and the consciousness' reasoning capacity.

Coronochakra: located in the upper region of the head, facing upwards. It is related to the most advanced thoughts and with the mentalsoma itself, which will be discussed below. There is a hypothesis that the halo of people called "saints" and the so-called state of enlightenment, or *samadhi*, are directly related to the expansion of energies of this chakra.

Remember that each of the chakras mentioned can be known by other names, in different lines of knowledge, especially oriental ones. As we mentioned in the chapter about nomenclature, some of the ideas of conscientiology are not exclusive to it, although having merit due to linking propositions in a scientific, logical and rational manner.

In addition to the 7 main chakras mentioned, there are several other minor chakras. These include: *plantochakras* (located in the sole of the feet, related to the absorption of energies), *palmochakras* (located in the palm of the hands, related to the exteriorization of energies) and *nuchochakra* (located in the nuchal region, related to energetic couplings).

It is important to note that chakras are very dynamic in their manifestation, acting uninterruptedly in the exchange of energies with different environments and people. Within conscientiology, the color of the chakras is secondary information, due to its fugacity, and its indirect association with the quality of the energies.

Mastery of the energosoma is of utmost importance for the consciousness to manifest themselves in the freest and most adequate way in this dimension. A consciousness that does not master their energies will always have difficulty living well, as they will tend to be swallowed by the energies from the environment or other consciousnesses. In this case, a basic law prevails "the energy of the greatest swallows that of the smallest".

4.1.2.2. BASIC MOBILIZATION OF ENERGIES (BME)

To develop practical control over one's energies, there are several procedures, and among them, a set of 3 basic techniques, called the *basic mobilization of energies* (BME), which is apparently simple, yet capable of changing a person's entire existence for the better.

Before addressing these techniques, it is important to note that bioenergies obey acts of the consciousness' will. Just as you close and open your hand, through the power of your will, you can also act upon your bioenergies as it suits you.

Needless to say, there is no need to apply any artifice from one's imagination to work with energies, it is enough that the consciousness is predisposed to feel and move them.

It's possible that at first you may have some difficulty, as sometimes decades of life have passed without ever having consciously performed an energetic mobilization. Just insist on applying the techniques presented below, so that, in a short amount of time, you will begin to increasingly perceive the energies, leaving no doubt about their existence and the possibility of achieving self-mastery.

Maintain your critical judgment and avoid forcing the perception something you are not actually feeling. Remember, as explained above, always apply the *principle of disbelief.*

Performing the BME:

1. Closed circulation of energies: activation of the flow of energies from the top of the head to the feet, and back up and down again, numerous times, in an accelerating rhythm. Begin through the force of your will (this alone is enough, command your energies) concentrate energies at the top of your head. After initiate the movement of this block of energies over and within your body, until reaching your feet. Then, move the energies in the opposite direction, from the feet to the head, and so on, in an uninterrupted, successive, and increasingly faster manner.

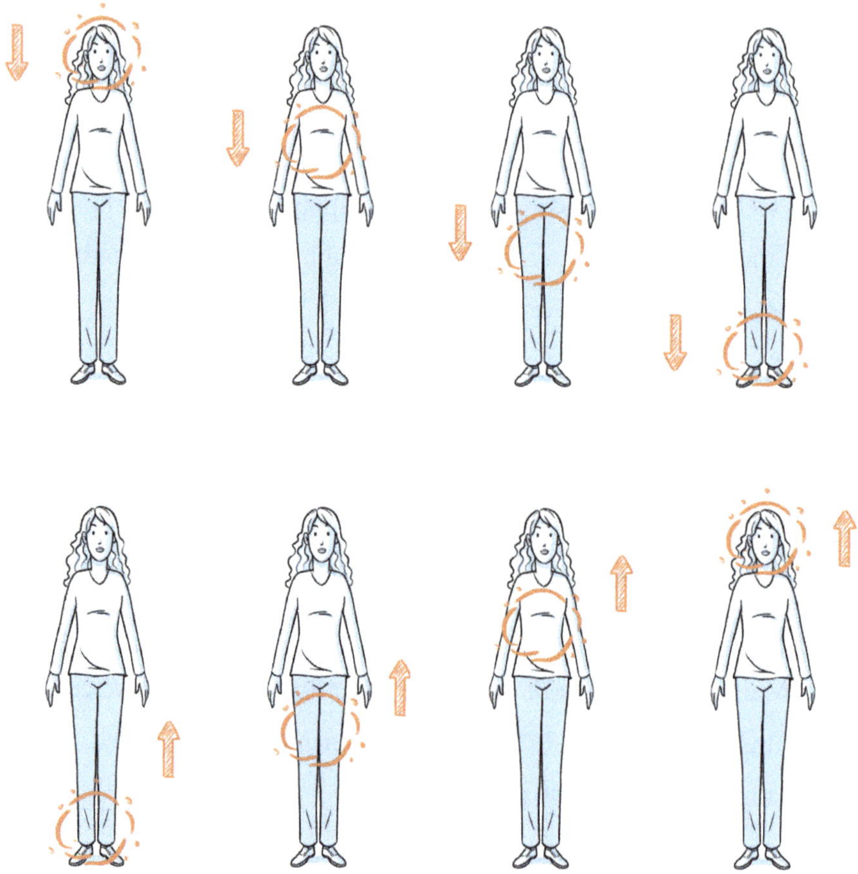

Figure 4. Closed circulation of energies.

It is interesting to note, that with time and increasing control over the maneuver, the energies tend to acquire their own vibratory pattern, whereby one no longer to needs to order them to go from head to toe, and vice versa, because they gain a "life of their own". This condition is given the technical name of *vibrational state* (VS), which is extremely important in energetic practices, because, when reached, a self-cleaning of the energosoma occurs.

In this case, any negative energies that may be with you tend to be automatically expelled. Therefore, the VS enables a state of energetic self-defense for as long as it lasts, that is, energies do not enter or leave the consciousness. In general, the VS is recognized, by those who apply it, as a state of extreme wellbeing, sometimes accompanied by pleasant tingles along the spine or throughout the body. And, of course, energy perceptions may vary from person to person. This technique is truly quite simple to apply, yet is both fascinating and impactful when self-demonstrated. Try experimenting it yourself!

Figure 5. Vibrational state (VS).

2. Exteriorization of Energies: This is a technique in which you, also through the strength of your will, command your energy to go out, from the entire body, in every direction. The intensity and speed of this exteriorization of energies is determined by you. If you wish, you can exteriorize from some specific part (e.g. from the palmochakras, through the palms of your hands).

You may have heard of reiki techniques, *healing passes* at a spiritist center, or energization work done by *laying on of hands*, among numerous other practices. All these activities work with the exteriorization of energies. What is different about the technique used in conscientiology is that one does not need to resort to prayers or other crutches to move them. You just need to propel your energies out from you; it's that simple. Give it a try.

This technique is especially important when you provide help to others by exteriorizing your best energies. Ideally, in this case, always make sure that you are feeling well. To do this, you can first apply the before mentioned VS technique.

There is also no need to worry about donating too much of your energies during the assistance, as they are inexhaustible. While giving energy, you are also automatically absorbing it through the entire energosoma.

Figure 6. Exteriorization of energies.

3. Absorption of energies: a technique that is part of the *basic mobilization of energies (BME)*, through which the inverse process of exteriorization is realized: by applying your will, you now pull in and absorb energies from the outside, you can do this throughout the body or in some specific part, if you wish.

The intensity and speed of this absorption of energies is always determined by you. This technique is especially indicated for energetic recomposition, generally after an exteriorization of energies.

Although the normalization of energies occurs naturally, as part of the paraphysiology of the energosoma, the fact is that we can greatly accelerate the recovery of our energies by applying this technique.

Figure 7. Absorption of energies.

4.1.2.3. GENERAL GUIDELINES OF THE BME

Very common perceptions had when activating one's energies include: itching, tingling, balloonment (sensation of the expansion of energies, as if you were bigger than you really are), sounds, increased sensitivity to influences from the surrounding environment, among others. These sensations are usually fleeting and disappear soon after ceasing the technique. If you notice any discomfort – which is rare – do not worry, as sometimes, this sensation can indicate an unblocking in the flow of energies.

Remember that you already use your energies in everyday life, but most of the time in an unconscious way. When you go to a place with vibrant nature and feel good, you naturally absorb energies from that environment. On the other hand, when you arrive at a certain place and feel bad, sometimes even because of unexpectedly encountering another person, you may be absorbing energies, which in this case, are generally not so good – and therefore you feel a malaise. In other words, you already apply energy techniques in your daily life, however the ideal is to move them consciously and autonomously.

The phenomenon of energy fields connecting is quite common and has gradations. When there is simple contact between the auras of two people, this is called *auric coupling*. When the connection intensifies, it is known as *sym*pathetic *as*similation (symas), and can reach the point where one person perceives exactly what the other is feeling.

The opposite of *symas* is *sym*pathetic *deas*similation (symdeas), performed through the, already discussed, important Vibrational State (VS) technique, which, through an intensification of energies, can generate, as already mentioned, an advanced state of energetic self-defense.

Another suggestion is that you initially apply these techniques in quieter places, such as at home, sitting comfortably on the couch, or even in bed. This can facilitate the perception of energy at the beginning. With time, you will be able to move your energy in any place or situation.

Figure 8. Auric coupling.

Figure 9. Sympathetic assimilation (symas): intensification of auric coupling.

4.1.3. PSYCHOSOMA

4.1.3.1. LUCID PROJECTION

Lucid projection is one of the most studied experiences within the universe of projectiology (the science dedicated to researching projections of the consciousness), which today encompasses the analysis of more than 40 types of parapsychic phenomena.

For example, it is very common to hear reports, in our conscientiology courses, from people who have woken in the middle of the night and had difficulty moving, as if they were trapped inside their body. That is, they are lucid and awake, but unable to move their soma. We call this phenomenon *catalepsy.*

Discarding any causes of physical origin (such as neurological problems), the fact is that projective catalepsy exists, it has an extraphysical origin and arises due to the involuntary discoincidence of the consciousness' vehicles of manifestation, resulting in the difficulty to physically move. When this occurs, just remain calm and focus on making a small movement, such as wiggling a fingertip or opening your eyes. Soon after, the you will recover movement of the entire body.

Another common example is to hear sounds inside your head (sometimes pops, clicks, or as if opening Velcro), especially when you are drifting off to sleep. The origin of these intracranial sounds may be linked to effects from the discoincidence of the bodies.

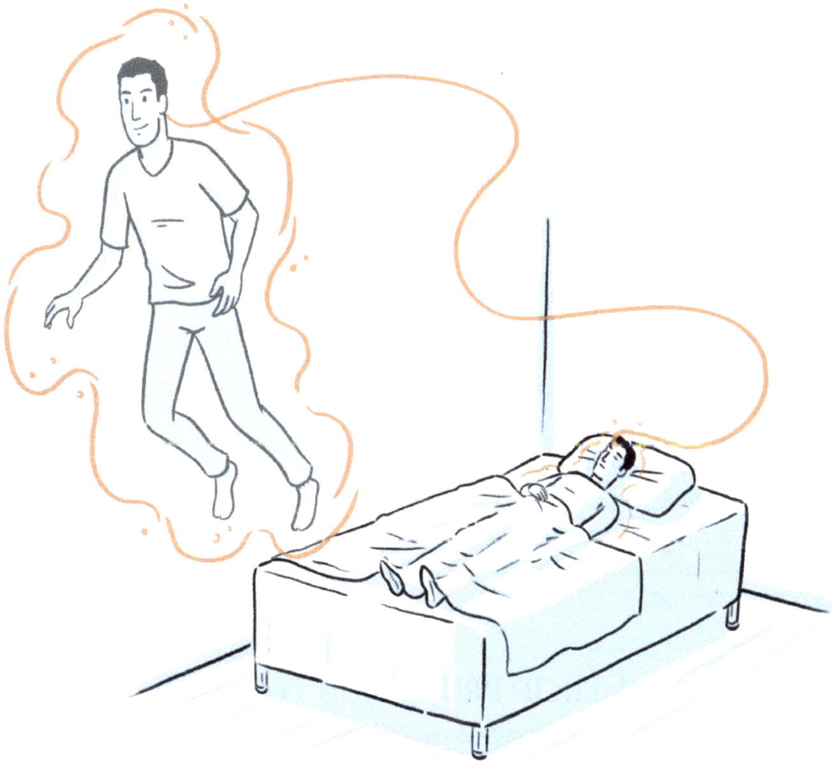

Figure 10. Lucid projection (LP).

It's important to note that the phenomenon of lucid projection should not be confused with sleep, nor the dream state. In a lucid projection, just like ordinary physical wakefulness (the state when a person is awake), you can do things, talk with other people, and gain knowledge. However, you are manifesting in another dimension – in this case extraphysical – and realize that the "I" exists independently from the physical body. This is truly an impactful reality, that inevitably brings profound changes to the life of the consciousness. During these experiences, you can even meet people who have died and speak with them, if this sparks your curiosity. It all depends on your level of preparation and determination.

Altered states of consciousness (ASC) are all those states that differ from the standard pattern of the ordinary physical waking state, they can be quite varied but are distinct from each other. Sleep and dreams are examples of ASCs, however lucid projection is another state, quite distinct from these. In a dream, the consciousness appears to be guided, and does not perform acts through their own will. They are "experienced" through the, generally illogical and irrational, dream. In a lucid projection, there is reasoning, logic and rationality. Therefore, the individual acts consciously, in the same way they experience the intraphysical dimension, but with much greater freedom of action.

4.1.3.2. LUCID PROJECTION TECHNIQUE

Lucid projection can occur spontaneously, but it can also be provoked through dozens of techniques to lucidly leave the physical body, each with numerous variations. For those who want more information, see the citation referring to the treatise *Projectiology* at the end of this book.

We will now present a technique that usually produces good results when applied. This is the projective technique of rhythmic breathing, which basically consists in increasing the proportion of carbon dioxide in the bloodstream, in a harmless way, through the control of one's breathing. It is recommended for people who are in good health, have regular checkups and do not have any serious cardiac problem.

It consists of lying down and mentally counting how long it takes to breathe in. Then, calmly and without forcing anything, hold your breath for 4 times the time it takes you to inhale, and exhaling for twice the amount of this inhalation time. If necessary, adjust these parameters to your particular case, so as not to overdo it. These steps should be repeated 10 times in a row.

An example: let's suppose that you mentally count that it took 4 seconds to inhale. Try to retain the air inside the lungs for 16 seconds and exhale for 8 seconds. Repeating this procedure 10 times, typically you will feel a light numbness and calmness that facilitates the discoincidence of your vehicles. You may stop perceiving the soma, as if it does not exist or had sunk into the bed. After this, it is just a small step to leaving the body. Relax and allow yourself to become free, disconnecting from your soma, and using the psychosoma to manifest yourself.

Allow me to quote a small phrase from page 133 of the book 700 Conscientiology Experiments, by Waldo Vieira, which illustrates this point well:

> "Knowing the precise time to *shift mental gears,* either when you must cease concentrating or when you must concentrate, constitutes a key to voluntary conscious projection. This includes the psychosoma's lucid take-off, for instance, and projections with continuous lucidity."

Sometimes, you may not be completely successful the first time you try this technique, and it may take a few days to reach this goal. However, you can be sure that the more you apply it, the closer you will be to lucidly producing the phenomenon, and this act will be very worthwhile.

Even if you do have a lucid projection, the quality of your sleep tends to be much better due to the relaxation produced. Have no fear. If in doubt, you can use the already recommended *basic mobilization of energies* (BME), before starting to apply the technique to lucidly leave the physical body.

Lucid projections bring countless benefits, which include both private and public ones. For example: therapeutic (for curing or alleviating illnesses); parapsychic (development of paraperceptions); psychological (increasing self-confidence); educational (promoting new learning). But, above all it serves to increase one's self-knowledge, which is indispensable for the evolution of the consciousness.

In order to study the different themes that exist within the mother-science or leader-science that is conscientiology, certain specialties are being structured, such as projectiology and from them, *Conscientiocentric Institutions* (CIs), each one with its own focus of activity.

At the end of this book, the interested reader will be able to find a brief presentation of each of the CIs within conscientiology, who can then be contacted in order to deepen the level of knowledge about them.

4.1.4. MENTALSOMA

As explained earlier, the *mentalsoma*, also known as the mental body or the body of ideas, among many other names, is considered, in conscientiology, as the most advanced vehicle of manifestation we are aware of at our current evolutionary stage.

It is possible, as far as we can understand today, for the consciousness to manifest itself only through the mentalsoma, detached from all the other bodies (soma, energosoma, and psychosoma). When this occurs, the manifestation of the consciousness is so subtle that we could consider it to be one's own essence.

Although quite evolved, it is possible to have lucid projections through the mentalsoma. Therefore, such a projection is a feasible reality for anyone sufficiently motivated.

Every type of activity that uses the intellect, in some way, contributes to mastering this advanced body, as it develops attributes related to it, such as: mental concentration, attention, prioritization, creativity, and association of ideas, among others.

Within the evolutionary scale of consciousness, with the passage of centuries and intraphysical lives, a consciousness tends to deactivate the other vehicles that constitute the holosoma and begins to act exclusively through the mentalsoma. That is, it becomes a *Free Consciousness*, one free from the action of matter, due to no longer needing the other bodies for its manifestation.

4.1.5. INTERVEHICULAR RELATIONSHIPS

It is important to note that there are profound interrelations between the bodies (vehicles) that compose the holosoma (soma, energosoma, psychosoma, and mentalsoma). It is not so difficult to theoretically explain how symbiosis occurs between the consciousness' vehicles of manifestation. However, in practice, it is not always easy to distinguish to what extent one body is manifesting itself and to what extent another one is acting, given they are constantly interfused in our daily life.

For example: if a physical illness occurs, there is no doubt that the tendency will be for the other bodies to be affected. If the consciousness has a pathological thought (mentalsoma), this will affect the individual's emotions (psychosoma) and, as a consequence, their energies (energosoma) too, and it may even materialize into some physical illness (soma). On the other hand, just one positive thought can reverberate throughout the consciousness' entire life. In other words, the holosoma is a set of bodies that intermingle and interpenetrate each other, with one influencing the other.

4.2. MULTIDIMENSIONALITY

For conscientiology, there is not just one existential dimension (that is, this physical dimension). There are infinite dimensions in which the consciousness manifests themselves in the extraphysical condition.

An interesting analogy that we could make would be with a gradient color scale, with a gradual modification of hues in which, for example, the color red turns into yellow, that turns into green, then blue, and so on. We have difficulties in determining the exact location in which one color stops and another starts, as they are interconnected.

Figure 11. Color *gradient*: an analogy of the interplay of consciential dimensions.

The consciential dimensions interpenetrate one another according to the vibratory pattern of energies that compose them. Corresponding to the integral vibratory pattern of the holosoma's energies (given every object in the universe has its own vibrational pattern, that is, a wave of manifestation according to physics, which gives rise to the phenomenon of *resonance*, among others), one of the bodies will have greater affinity with this or that extraphysical dimension.

Therefore, it is stated that, where there is one *physical finger*, there are also infinite other *fingers* manifesting in multiple joint dimensions.

Conscientiology considers that 3 basic states of the consciousness exist:

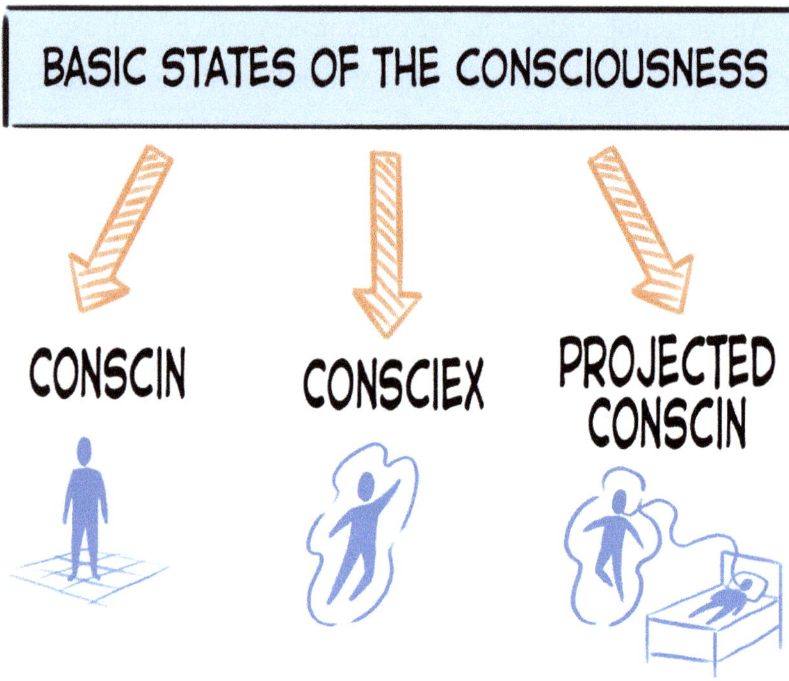

Figure 12. Basic states of the consciousness.

1. Conscin: *in*traphysical *consc*iousness (in this case, a consciousness manifesting in this intraphysical dimension with the physical body, that is, they possess a soma).

2. Consciex: *ex*traphysical *consci*ousness (in this case, a consciousness manifesting in the extraphysical dimension without connection to a physical body, that is without a soma, commonly known as a "disincarnated" or "spirit").

1. Projected Conscin: third condition, a transition, when a conscin manifests themselves in the extraphysical dimension, having left the physical body resting in the intraphysical dimension. This condition is popularly referred to as "unfolding" or "astral projection" and is technically known as lucid projection (LP).

4.3. EXISTENTIAL SERIALITY

Perhaps the reader has already deduced this, but let's make it clear: from the perspective of conscientiology, no one came into existence the moment they are born, or *soma*tically *re*activate (resoma), nor do they cease to exist the moment they die, or *soma*tically *de*activate (desoma). Every consciousness is the result of the sum of choices made over many lifetimes.

It works, therefore, with the principle of multiple lives, "reincarnations" or a series of existences, starting from the idea that this life is just *one more* in the evolutionary trajectory of the consciousness.

In theory every consciousness can access their past lives. This paraphenomenon is given the specific name *retrocognition* (memory of or access to past experiences), which can be technically developed and generated.

Lucidity about past lives can be important, for example, to avoid making the same mistakes or to better understand the situations and relationships in which we find ourselves today and are related to our past.

The important thing, in this case, is for the consciousness to prove to *themselves* the existence of other lives and its influences in their current life, while always maintaining critical thinking and applying the previously discussed *principle of disbelief*.

5. ADVANCED THEMES IN CONSCIENTIOLOGY

Next, we will briefly explain some of the advanced topics covered by conscientiology, as a kind of *intellectual apertif.*

Rather than approaching the subject in an exhaustive way, the objective is to just *outline* a topic, seeking to arouse the reader's curiosity.

Although there are *thousands* of topics, we have selected some considered of greatest interest, approaching them in an introductory manner with this book.

5.1. THOSENE

In conscientiology, everything that we think generates some kind of sentiment (feeling), which in turn generates some kind of energy. The union of these 3 concepts, is called *thosene* (= *tho*ught + *sen*timent + *ene*rgy)

It is an inseparable manifestation, usually not perceived because it is automatic, but the fact is that, in practice, everything that we think, ultimately, creates some pattern of energy.

The set of thosenes, known as *holothosene* (*holo* = all, set, whole; *thosene* = *tho*ught + *sen*timent + *ene*rgy), existing at different scales, is the average pattern of thoughts of a certain person or environment. The tendency is always for a holothosene to be in tune with similar patterns, based on the law *like attracts like.*

There are diverse categories or types of thosenes, which can be classified according to the idea they predominantly express. For the interested reader, you will find some of them in the glossary at the end of this book, such as: *graphothosene, materthosene, orthothosene, neothosene, retrothosene and pathothosene.*

Although it seems a simple concept, reflecting on the practical repercussions of the thosene can cause profound changes in the life of any person.

Through self-awareness of the importance of personal thoughts, you begin to take better care of the quality of your thosenes, which are reflected throughout one's existence. Providing a straighter evolution, without so many problems and with greater evolutionary utility.

5.2. PROEXIS

Conscientiology considers that nobody comes to life just for tourism or leisure. We all come with something to do, with tasks ranging from the simpler to the more complex. This so-called life mission is given the name *exis*tential *pro*gram (proexis).

When a consciousness identifies and is doing what they came to do in this existence, they tend to feel extremely happy within themselves and that each day is worth living, because they perceive their evolutionary progress.

On the other hand, when the consciousness doesn't identify or do their proexis, the tendency is for them to experience melancholy, despondency, dejection, depression and numerous other problems so common today. The person notices that their life is at a standstill, almost without any value and usefulness.

Hence the importance for each consciousness to identify what they came to do in this life, to walk in the right direction and assume their own evolution.

In general, retrieving one's proexis and recovering the meaning of human existence, depends on assisting other consciousnesses. We came to intraphysical life primarily to serve one another, that is, it is through helping other people, and feeling useful, that a consciousness can improve their self-esteem and recover their role in the cosmos or, to put it another way, fulfil their role as a *mini*piece in the evolutionary *maxi*mechanism.

5.3. INTERMISSIVE COURSE

From a conscientiological point of view, a consciousness does not remain in limbo between one life and another. They continue in their activities, even if unaware they no longer have a physical body (soma).

During this time between one intraphysical existence and another, the *intermissive period* (between life missions), there is the possibility of experiencing a kind of preparation, like taking a course, to increase the chances of success in the fulfillment of their proexis.

This specific preparation is known as an *Intermissive Course* (IC) and in this case, who participates in this activity during the intermissive period is called an *intermissivist.*

Participating in an IC increases the person's responsibility to use their intraphysical life in a beneficial way. They intimately recognize there is something important to be done. They wish to contribute to the evolution of other beings and to the improvement of the universe in which they manifest.

5.4. HOLOMATURITY

The main objective of conscientiology is to promote the self-evolution of a consciousness, but this is only acquired through the gradual achievement of integral maturity in relation to every injunction and context of existence.

It is when experiencing a difficult moment that the person has the opportunity to practically demonstrate what level of lucidity and evolution they have already achieved. The study and practice of advanced themes gives impetus to the consciousness' evolutionary process.

The composition of holomaturity is achieved through the improvement of *self*-organization and other acts performed by themselves ("*self*"), such as: *self*-familiarity, *self*-determination, *self*-confidence, *self*-development, *self*-liberation, *self*-realization, *self*-discipline, *self*-sufficiency, *self*-examination, *self*-awareness, among other acts.

There are tools for measuring these attributes, among which the *Conscientiogram* stands out. It is a work aimed at self-evaluation and self-judgment in relation to a series of traits that comprise an integrated personality.

This tool also takes into account the existence of the consciousness known as *Homo sapiens serenissimus*, or Serenissimus. They are considered a feasible evolutionary model of full maturity for this planet. A Serenissimus being is the benchmark who beneficially uses 100% of each consciential attribute analyzed by the *Conscientiogram*.

5.5. COSMOETHICS

Conscientiology studies a greater ethics present in the entire cosmos, called *cosmoethics*. Cosmoethics is the multidimensional cosmic morality, situated beyond social and intraphysical morality. Its understanding and application is deeply correlated to the level of maturity already attained by the consciousness and is revealed in every act of their multidimensional conduct.

In other words, it acts like a regulatory mechanism of consciential evolution, a set of cosmic laws that govern the evolution of all beings that constitute the universe. All consciousnesses are subject to its application, whether aware of it or not.

Sometimes, it is simplistically considered as the *law of cause and effect*, a topic explored in many lines of knowledge. However, strictly speaking, this is only one result of applying cosmoethics, a superior concept.

Applying cosmoethics begins with the simple idea that in our lives we get back what we offer to the universe. That is, if we act on behalf of assistance, the good, and truly without secondary interests, the tendency will be towards evolutionary growth in a virtuous cycle, within the *flow of the cosmos*.

Upon attaining higher levels on the evolutionary scale, a consciousness starts to encompass principles and values that increasingly consider assistance to others, rather than those that only appeal to their ego.

When the opposite occurs and we act against this reality, becoming aware of having committed an error, we reap the undesirable crop of what, ultimately, we ourselves sowed.

5.6. RECIN

Through the discovery of holomaturity and cosmoethics, it is inevitable that a consciousness interested in evolving review their own postures, starting with their *thosenes*, a topic already discussed. This is the beginning of an action we call *recin*, a neologism originating from the fusion of the words: *rec*ycling + *in*traconsciential.

In other words, the person begins to question and reconsider their thoughts and attitudes, always seeking the best evolutionary perspective, which implies a centrifugal, intimate reform, one from the *inside out*.

The depth and repercussions of recin depend on how much the person wants to act on aspects in which they have greater difficulty, through their own personal will. The impact of this change of posture is varied, and can have repercussions in the person's family, circle of friends, and even at work.

Conscientiology presents countless techniques to produce recins. One main technique is to promote the identification of weaktraits (weaktraits: difficulties, what we have to improve) and to use our strongtraits (strongtraits: abilities, what we have already developed) for this purpose.

Hence, the great value of conscientiometry tools (the conscientiology specialty dedicated to the metric study of the consciousness) and conscientiotherapy resources (the conscientiology specialty dedicated to the integral treatment of the consciousness).

5.7. PENTA

One of the ways to contribute to the improvement of everyone's existence is to apply the advanced technique of *penta*, an acronym formed from the combination of the words *pe*rsonal, *en*ergetic and *ta*sk.

Penta is one of the advanced techniques of conscientiology in which a conscin, essentially, proposes to donate their energies every day for about 50 minutes, at a specific place and time, to help other consciousnesses.

Besides being a great interassistantial tool, above all it serves as self-help, because the conscin first seeks to balance themselves, before assisting others.

Through the transfer of more balanced and homeostatic energies, it is possible to treat various types of problems, from physical illnesses, emotional issues, relationships, among many others.

The technique is performed under the supervision of an extraphysical consciousness, in this case a technical function-specific helper, who helps the conscin apply and develop their penta.

It is worth remembering that the technical helper is a consciousness who knows about the subject and has mastered the best way to help. This differs therefore from consciousnesses, popularly known as "guardian angels", "spiritual guides", "mentors", and many other names, who do not necessarily have the technical mastery over this set of procedures.

It is important to clarify that penta is a set of specific procedures, and as such requires preparation. For those who are interested in the subject, at the end of this book there is a list of books that address this theme, especially *Penta Manual*, authored by Waldo Vieira.

5.8. CONSCIENTIAL BOND

Many people have significantly improved their lives after adopting conscientiology's evolutionary techniques in their daily lives.

Hundreds of thousands of people have already participated in lectures and courses held in dozens of *Conscientiocentric Institutions* (CIs), who have been developing the leading science of conscientiology.

Many of these people wish to do something with this knowledge which has helped them so much.

A practical way to assist in the dissemination of conscientiology is to volunteer at one of the CIs that work to expand the science.

In this context, the concept of *consciential bond* appears, that is, a connection to ideas and not the financial or employment side of things.

Today, there are thousands of volunteers who generously donate their time and energies towards assistantial tasks within CIs. You can find the *List of CIs* available at the end of this book.

5.9. COGNOPOLIS

Around the planet many conscientiology volunteers with a consciential bond are creating cities of knowledge, known as *Cognopolis*, which are like oases for the development of these ideas.

Among them the *Foz do Iguaçu Cognopolis* stands out, which today is a district officially recognized by the Brazilian municipality, and which had thousands of consciousnesses involved in its construction. Dr. Waldo Vieira, a pioneer in the systemization of conscientiology and author of several treatises and other significant books, lived there until 2015, being fully active in his studies until he desomated at the age of 83.

At this Cognopolis, several *Conscientiocentric Institutions* (CIs) have *campuses*, each with their own specialties, laboratories and area for debates and discussions; a hotel with 300 beds; and many residential complexes where volunteers live.

Among all the projects hosted in this "city of knowledge", the construction and maintenance of the *Holotheca Cultural Megacenter* is highlighted. This project was designed by renowned architect Oscar Niemeyer, and will be a reference for raising the cultural level of the entire region. If interested, you are invited to know more about and assist in the materialization of this megaproject.

On the internet, you will find more information about it. Therefore, here, we will limit ourselves to this brief overview (www.conscienciologia.org.br; www.tertuliaconscienciologia.org). However, for now, we reinforce our invitation for you to come and visit us.

5.10. SPECIALTIES OF CONSCIENTIOLOGY

As seen so far, conscientiology is a very comprehensive science. In this introductory discussion we only presented some basic concepts. There is far greater knowledge organized in the dozens of treatises, not to mention the hundreds of other already published works.

For you to have an idea, conscientiology currently involves more than 1000 specialties and subspecialties (for more information, see the *Encyclopedia of Conscientiology*), with each theme having its own nomenclature and research, hence the need for specialization.

In the same way that medicine has various specialties (such as cardiology, angiology, gynecology, urology, neurology, occupational medicine and many others), conscientiology also has its specialties, such as proexology (dedicated to the proexis), projectiology (which studies consciential projections), seriexology (which researches the seriexis – existential seriation or successive lives), pentology (which develops the penta technique), paraphenomenology (which investigates paraphenomena), and many others.

For each subfield, there are publications, specific courses and many *Conscientiocentric Institutions* (CIs) studying these specialties and seeking to expand them, as you can find noted in the references at the end of this book.

5.11. ENCYCLOPEDIA OF CONSCIENTIOLOGY

Today, the *Encyclopedia of Conscientiology* is in full development, and already its 9th printed edition contains: 4,580 verbets (entries), 23,004 pages and 702 authors (Base year: 2018). Its pages cover in detail, thorough a systematized methodology, all the themes that constitute the universe of this new science, that is, strictly speaking, an activity without an end.

Every day, a new verbet is presented, functioning like a free long-term course, through the site www.tertuliaconscienciologia.org. This activity is very important for systematizing knowledge and expanding conscientiology specialties.

We invite you to watch conscientiological tertulias through the site www.tertuliaconscienciologia.org and moreover become, even at a distance, a *Friend of the Encyclopedia*, a project which makes it possible to materially support the development of this work. For more information about the Encyclopedia of Conscientiology and the program *Friends of the Encyclopedia*, visit www.enciclopediadaconscienciologia.org.

BOOK-TALK EPILOGUE

As can be seen, conscientiology is a very broad science that has numerous strands and correlations with various other sciences and specialties.

It is a study deepened every day, through the publication of new works that complement the research realized by thousands of active volunteers.

The objective of this book was to provide a general overview, without trying to be closed in anyway.

For more information, I suggest reading the treatises, books and other related sources mentioned in the list of books at the end of this work.

INVITATION

If you are interested in the themes presented in this book and would like to deepen your understanding of them, you are invited to refer to the *Conscientiocentric Institution's* (CIs) addresses listed on the following pages for more information. The *websites* mentioned provide extensive material and most associations offer a range of free activities for those wishing to begin their studies.

If you are interested in knowing more about this science, contact us with your questions, referring to this publication, and we will send you more information for free.

Feel free to contact us by email or at the address below. We have a large team of volunteer teachers who are able to give free talks in the major languages, on different topics, and we can visit your city to teach a course of interest.

If you visit Foz do Iguaçu, Brazil, come and see us. We have many conscientiology activities occurring within Cognopolis – a district of knowledge – which is constantly being developed and expanded.

Contact:

AIEC – International Association for the Expansion of Conscientiology

Av. Felipe Wandscheer, 6.200 – bairro Cognópolis

Foz do Iguaçu – PR – Brasil – CEP 85.856-530

Author's email: cesarcordioli@gmail.com

ACKNOWLEDGMENT

Lastly, for you who made it this far, we thank you for your time. And, we hope the information provided here has been of some value to your existence.

Until next time.

The Author

BIBLIOGRAPHICAL REFERENCES

Vieira, Waldo(Org.); ***Enciclopédia da Conscienciologia;*** Digital; reviewers ENCYCLOSSAPIENS Reviewer Team; 23,188p.; gloss. 5,480 terms (verbets); 701 microbiographies; alph.; 9th. Ed revised and expanded.; *International Association of the Encyclopedia of Conscientiology* (ENCYCLOSSAPIENS); & *International Association Editares;* Foz do Iguaçu, PR; 2018.

Idem; *Manual da Proéxis: Programação Existencial;* 168 p.; 40 caps.; 17 refs.; alph.; 21x14cm; br.; 3ªEd.; Instituto Internacional de Projeciologia; Rio de Janeiro, RJ; 2003.

Idem; *Manual da Tenepes: Tarefa Energética Pessoal*; 138p.; 34 chaps.; 147 abbrevs.; gloss. 282 terms; 5 refs.; alph.; 21x14cm; br.; International Institute of Projectiology; Rio de Janeiro, RJ; 1995.

Idem; *Nossa Evolução;* 168p.; 15 chaps.; 149 abbrevs.; glos.282terms; 6refs.; alph.; 21x14cm; br.; International Institute of Projectiology; Rio de Janeiro, RJ; 1996.

Idem; *Projeciologia: Panorama das Experiências da Consciência Fora do Corpo Humano;* 1,248p.; 525 chaps.; 150 abbrevs.; 43 illus.; 5 indexes; 1 synopsis; gloss. 300 terms; 2,041 refs.; alph.; geo.; ono.; 28 x 21 x 7 cm; bdg.; 4th Ed. revised and expanded; International Institute of Projectiology; Rio de Janeiro, RJ; 1999.

Idem; *Projeções da Consciência: Diário de Experiências Fora do Corpo Físico;* 224p.; gloss. 25 terms; alph.; 21x14cm; br.; 8thEd revised; International Association Editares; Foz do Iguaçu, PR; 2008.

Idem; *700 Experimentos da Conscienciologia;* 1.058 p.; 700 chaps.; 147 abbrevs.; 600 enums.; 8 indexes; 2 tabs.; 300 tests; gloss. 280 terms; 5,116 refs.; alph.; geo.; ono.; 28.5x21.5x7cm; bdg.; *International Institute of Projectiology;* Rio de Janeiro, RJ; 1994.

TABLE OF FIGURES

GLOSSARY OF CONSCIENTIOLOGY TERMS

The current glossary was developed based on concepts presented by the researcher Waldo Vieira (1932–2015) in the scientific Treatises *700 Conscientiology Experiments* (1994), *Projectiology: A Panorama of Experiences of the Consciousness Outside the Human Body* (1999), *Homo sapiens reurbanisatus* (2004), *Homo sapiens pacificus* (2007), *Encyclopaedia of Conscientiology* (2013), and *Dicionário de Argumentos da Conscienciologia* (*Dictionary of Arguments of Conscientiology*) (2014).

Absentrait – A trait missing in the personality of a human being, in this case a strongtrait which would enable this conscin to complete with reasonable success their current proexis, and is in the range of their current evolutionary level. This missingtrait can be identified through conscientiometric study.

Ambientex – Extraphysical ambience, or extraphysical environment is the place where a projected conscin manifests out of its human body and beyond the tridimensional geographic world, sphere, intraphysical, material, or human dimension of the ordinary physical waking state.

Anticosmoethics – Immature positioning in which a consciousness consciously or unconsciously infringes the universal correct, evolutionary principles of multidimensional cosmoethics, acting in an unworthy, antifraternal, marginal, or criminal way, with pathological or malicious effects.

Apriorismosis – Is the quality, condition, or state of chronic apriorism of a conscin only able to reason *a priori,* based on previous fixed elements, without examination, analysis, or verification, regardless of facts or parafacts.

Assistantiology – Specialty of conscientiology that studies the techniques of interconsciential assistance and support, notably as regards their effects on the consciousness considered as a "whole", holosomatic and multimillennial, with a view to its holomaturity; a work of lucid solidarity between consciousnesses on their way to megafraternity. It constitutes a scientific subfield of conviviology.

Baratrosphere – Is the pathological extraphysical dimension of the Earth's paratroposphere, used as the collective home of anticosmoethical, unhealthy, parapsychotic, and paracomatose consciexes.

Charisma – The magnetism, or human electricity coming from a person's psychosphere or specific holothosene, composing their set of thosenic holosomatic manifestations, notably with the consciential energies they exteriorise, either consciously or unconsciously, influencing cosmoethically or anticosmoethically this and other consciential dimensions.

CI – *See Conscientiocentric Institution.*

Clairaudience – Capacity related to auditory parapsychic conscins, sensitive listeners, or clairaudients, able to perceive, or receive telepathic messages, for them, and in this case sometimes audible, sent by consciexes and projected conscins.

Clairvoyance – Parapsychic capacity to capture, perceive, or feel a specific pattern of consciential energy, either from an object, environment, or consciousness located in the intraphysical or extraphysical dimension, being chronologically in the past, present, or future, and to transform this energetic perception into an image.

Claritask – Is the clarification task, or experience of the consciousness alert to rational, libertarian, scientific, and cosmoethical assistantiality done at a high level in favour of all consciousnesses.

Communex – Is the extraphysical community, parapopulation group, or reunion and life in common with other consciexes in a specific extraphysical dimension.

Complexis (existential completism) – Rare condition in which the exceptional pre-*serenissimus* consciousness manages to reasonably perform the attributions conferred to them for their life on Earth (proexis), taking advantage of the evolutionary potential offered by their soma.

Con – Hypothetical unit to measure the level of lucidity of a conscin or consciex.

Conscientiall bond – Is the cosmoethic self-lucid voluntary polykarmic bond that flourishes between a volunteer and a conscientiocentric institution or organisation.

Consciential continuism – Condition of wholeness, without gaps, in the continuity of consciential life through providential programming and evolutionary self-relay, that is, the amendment of the current life experience, the lives coming immediately before and after, incessantly, in a cohesive and unique whole, with a solution of continuity or watertight consciential experiences.

Consciential encapsulation – Is the energetic, paratechnical, and advanced manoeuvre of a lucid conscin experienced in mobilising consciential energies (CEs) in themselves or extraconscientially, promoting assistantial isolation and temporary energetic annulment of specifically intrusive thosenic manifestations. It can be performed individually or for a group of conscins and/or consciexes, either healthy or ill, and stems from the promoter's decisive will, strong and healthy intention and self-determination.

Consciential energy – Is the immanent energy employed by a consciousness in its thosenations or its general manifestations.

Consciential microuniverse – Is the consciousness *per se*, understood as a whole, and encompassing all its attributes, thosenes, and manifestations in the development of its evolution; the microcosmos of the consciousness related to the macrocosmos of the universe.

Consciential openness – Advanced condition of the neophilic conscin with omnilateral opening of its self-thosenity to knowledge regarding the evolution of consciousness, capable of intentionally carrying out in their existence the advanced evolutionary techniques of conscientiology such as: cosmoethicology, invexis, penta, and deperticity.

Consciential paradigm – Is the leading theory of conscientiology, based on consciousness itself.

Consciential self-bilocation – Is the act of the intraphysical projector meeting and looking at their own human body face-to-face, their consciousness however being outside it and in another vehicle of consciential manifestation.

Conscientíal self-relay – Is the advanced condition in which a consciousness evolves by consecutively intertwining intraphysical lives, in the way of the links in a chain (seriexis) within this consciousness′ multiexistential cycle (holobiography).

Consciential wholesaling – System of individual behaviour characterised by the guideline of performing consciential acts together, without leaving behind evolutionary negative traces or gaps.

Conscientiocentric Institution (CI) – Is a centre where activities and self-research on consciousness and on consciential reeducation takes place. It has a corpus and totally transparent legal statutes, being intrinsically, cosmoethically, and consciencially healthy.

Conscientiogram – Technical spreadsheet of assessment and measurement of the level of evolution of a consciousness; the consciential megatest is modelled on the *Homo sapiens serenissimus,* who represents 100% of the evolutionary scale and is responsible for an exemplary positive egokarmic account.

Conscientiological *Tertulia* – Gathering, informal spontaneous meeting, or assembly of like-minded researchers to debate current themes, make quick analyses, and obtain transient consensus to their neo-researches, hypotheses, and theorices. In this 2-hour free daily Long-term-running Course, without pre-requisites, current novel theorical approaches and themes of interest to all, and either curricular or more advanced subjects in conscientiology are discussed.

Conscientiologist – Conscin engaged in the permanent study and objective experimentation within the field of research of conscientiology, in the quality of agent of evolutionary renovation (retrocognitive agent) in the libertarian work of all consciousnesses in general.

Conscientiology – Is the science that studies the consciousness in an integral, holosomatic, multidimensional, multimillennial, and multiexistential way, in its different states, and including its reactions before immanent energies and consciential energies.

Conscientiometrology – Is the speciality that studies the conscientiological assessment and measurement, or evaluation of a consciousness, using the resources and methods offered by conscientiology, capable of laying the possible basis for the mathematisation of the consciousness. Main instrument: the conscientiogram.

Consciex – Is the extraphysical consciousness, the paracitizen of the extraphysical society.

Conscin – Is the intraphysical consciousness when in the human body of either a man or woman.

Consecutive personality – Is a conscin with whom, in hetero-research, you interact in this human life in two different stages, the first being short when the personality desomates, and the second when the same personality resomates after a reasonably brief intermissive period.

Consoltask – Consolation task is the personal or group first assistantial task done in evolutionary interassistantiality to another consciousness.

Consreu – Is the extraphysical consciousness with compulsive misplaced pathological paragenetics, who in the course of the current extraphysical reurbanizations promoted by *Serenissimi* and evolutiologists, is transferred from the pathological extraphysical community (barathrosphere) where it has lived for centuries to this other transitional relatively more evolved extraphysical community. The idea is that consciousness can then prepare itself to resomate on Earth. In the more serious cases, the consciousness will undergo imposed transmigration to another planet of an inferior intraphysical level of evolution.

Cosmoconsciousness – A consciousness′ condition or inner perception of the cosmos, life, and order in the universe, in an intellectual and cosmoethical jubilation impossible to describe, when the consciousness feels the living presence of the universe and becomes one with it, in an indivisible unity.

Cosmoethical calculation – Set of procedures integrated by calculation, conjecture, detailed, and exhaustive evaluation to develop any individual or group.

Cosmoethics – Is the ethics of the cosmos, or the reflection on cosmic multidimensional morals, defining one′s consciential holomaturity. It goes beyond all social intraphysical morals, or any other morals presented under any human label, in the way of maximum moral and emotional discernment, arising from the intimacy of the microuniverse of each consciousness.

Cosmogram – Is a technical spreadsheet created to determine and evaluate the realities of the universe filtered by the multidimensional principles of conscientiology, using the maximum possible association of ideas for an overall view based on facts, reaching and involving the holothosene of the self and heterocritical conscin.

Cosmovisiology – Is the science applied to the theorical study of the evolutionary understanding of the conscientiological exhaustive, multidimensional, multiexistential, holothosenic, holomnemonic, holobiographical, holokarmic, and holosomatic cosmovision.

Deperticity – Evolutionary consciential quality of being deperto, or permanent and totally deintruded, while perfectly self-conscious of this condition when performing assistantial tasks benefitting other consciousnesses.

Deperto – Is the intraphysical being, or conscin, permanent and totally deintruded, perfectly self-conscious of their condition of deperticity.

Desoma – Deactivation of the soma that inevitably occurs to all conscins; final projection; first death; biological death; monothanatosis. This first desoma is simply the deactivation of one's human body, or soma. The second desoma, in turn, is the deactivation of a desomated conscin's energosoma. And the third desoma is the deactivation of a conscin's psychosoma.

Egokarma – Principle of cause and effect acting in a consciousness' evolution, when exclusively centred in its ego. State of free will linked to infantile egocentrism.

Egokarmology – Science applied to the specific, systematic, technical study and theatical knowledge, or the research of the structure, condition, or character of the relationships between the principles of cause and effect acting in the consciousness' evolution exclusively centred in its ego, in the universe of the law of action and reaction, law of eternal return, or holokarmalogy.

Energosoma – Is the energetic parabody of a conscin.

Energosomatics – Speciality of conscientiology applied to the study of the quality of the manifestations of the human consciousness (conscin) derived from the energosoma, or energetic parabody, as well as energetic manoeuvres, and their consequent influence on the self-thosenity and states of coincidence and discoincidence of that conscin.

Enerspring – the energetic spring, or energetic primetime; a more or less long lasting personal condition, the apex of a conscin's healthy and constructive consciential energies.

Equipex – Group of extraphysical experts tuned and interactive consciousnesses actively acting in interdimensional evolutionary enterprises.

Euphorex – Condition of extraphysical euphoria that occurs after somatic deactivation and stems from the feeling of having reasonably accomplished one's proexis; *post-mortem* euphoria; paraeuphoria; post-somatic euphoria.

Evolutient – An assisted conscin undergoing conscientiotherapy.

Evolutiologist – A supportive consciousness that becomes an intelligent coordinator of existential programmes (proexes) relative to the consciential evolution of several individuals or groups of consciousnesses from the supporter megagroupkarma.

Evolutiology – Specialty of conscientiology applied to the studies of consciousness evolution thoroughly addressed in an integral, holosomatic, multiexistential, and multidimensional manner. It is a scientific subfield of thosenology.

Evolutionary group – Gathering of more or less lucid consciousnesses evolving together, according to the affinity of their emotions, ideas, and acts.

Evolutionary intelligence – Is the capacity to perceive, learn, understand, and adapt to human life by applying the theatical self-conscious expansion of the mechanism of already integrated personal consciential evolution, there included: cosmoethicology, seriexology, and proexology. It evidences a consciousness' self-discernment regarding rational consciential evolution and lucid self-evolution, as well as it maximizes the consciousness' own cosmoethical self-thosenic performance.

Extraphysical Central of Energy (ECE) – Parainstitution specialised, planned, and set to stock, maintain, and monitor consciential energy (CE), as an extraphysical station of consciential energies, with the objective of supplying and distributing homeostatic therapeutic energies for the efficient assistance to consciousnesses – consciexes and conscins – under the direct supervision of the Invisible College of *Serenissimi.*

Extraphysical Central of Fraternity (ECF) – Parainstitution, or extraphysical community specialised, planned, and set to irradiate manifestations or cosmothosenation of fraternity, permeating the cosmos in a therapeutic and homeostatic way, in a silent, anonymous, and efficient assistance to all consciousnesses in general.

Extraphysical Central of Veracity (ECV) – Parainstitution or extraphysical community specialised, planned, and set to irradiate manifestations or paraconstructs of basic truth, or veracity in the cosmos, therapeutic and homeostatic, in the efficient assistance to all consciousnesses in general.

Existential inverter – A human consciousness (or conscin) predisposed to use the technique of invexis in their current intraphysical life.

Existential recycler – A conscin who applies the evolved technique of existential recycling (recexis) in their current human life, envisaging to accelerate their evolution.

Existential recycling – *See Recexis.*

Existential self-mimicry – Is the imitation, on the part of a conscin, of their past experiences, either from their current intraphysical rebirth or from past lives.

Experimentology – Specialty of conscientiology applied to the technical studies of the evolutionary experiments of a consciousness in all its forms, nature, and categories.

Extraphysical help – Evident assistance (support, aid, backing, boost, reinforcement, lift; sustenance) received from extraphysical helpers capable of acting in a healthy, universalist, and non-manipulative manner, alongside the usual daily intraphysical manifestations of a conscin, when the latter already holds obvious cosmoethical merit, for the development and conclusion of their personal existential programme (maxiproexis).

Extraphysical – Relative to that which is out, or beyond the intraphysical or human state; a consciential state less physical than the soma.

Extraphysical clinic – *Commonly: Offiex. See Offiex.*

Extraphysical helper – Beneficial consciousness, helper of a human consciousness (conscin), or of several human consciousnesses at the same time, when related by their level of evolution, notably during extraphysical projections, encompassing the beneficial influence throughout the whole intraphysical life of a personality, and even during the ordinary, physical, waking state.

Extraphysical intruder – Is an extraphysical consciousness that promotes the pathological condition of extraphysical harassment, negative action, or insistent persecution, directly or indirectly, of any nature, on other consciousnesses.

Extraphysical reurbanization – *See Reurbex.*

Extraphysical transmigrationology – Science, or speciality of conscientiology applied to the study of the interplanetary transmigrations of extraphysical consciousnesses. These change their paraprovenance, establish a new intraphysical planetary domicile, with consciexes arriving all the time to this planet and leaving to other inhabited ones, under the guidance of evolutiologists and *Serenissimi.*

Extraphysicology – Specialty of conscientiology applied to the technical studies of the relationships and experiences of a conscin in other dimensions beyond intraphysicality.

Extrapolationism – Study applied to the experiences of extrapolations, or evolutionary sporadic anticipations, obviously neither usual nor mundane, on the part of a consciousness at any evolutionary level, in relation to their own current level, the one immediately above, or even a more advanced level.

Free Consciex – Is the extraphysical consciousness finally free (by deactivation of its psychosoma, or emotional parabody) from the series of human lives (seriexology), or consecutive intraphysical lives. This is an ancient multimillennial process and they stand, in the evolution hierarchy, right after the *Homo sapiens serenissimus,* as they start another yet more advanced evolutionary course, whose main guidelines are also as yet unknown to the current terrestrial humanity.

General homeostasis – Is the process of regulation through which cosmic life can be constantly maintained in a state of balance, or homeostasis between consciential principles.

Gescon – Is a conscin's evolutionary cosmoethical useful production, or the conscin's performance of works of a true fraternal nature,, based on libertarian neoideas, within the framework of the personal tasks of a more advanced and elaborate proexis.

Groupality – Quality of the evolutionary group of a consciousness; condition of the state of evolution of a group.

Groupkarma – Principle of cause and effect acting in a consciousness' evolution when centered in their evolutionary group. State of individual free will connected to the evolutionary group.

Groupkarmology – Specialty of conscientiology applied to the technical studies of relationships, or principles of cause and effect acting on the evolution of consciousness when centered on their evolutionary group (science of evolutionary groups; net of evolutionary relationships).

Groupkarmic adjustment – Is the karmic adjustment of someone when it occurs together and simultaneously with other conscins or consciexes.

Groupkarmic interprison – Is the coercive interconsciential commitment resulting from joint group anticosmoethical actions practised together in the past, leaving the consciousness now in the condition of groupkarmic inseparability from those very same evolutionary consciential principles, or consciousnesses from the past.

Guinea pig-conscin – Is the intraphysical conscin investigated, analysed, examined, anatomised, detailed, and cosmoethically used in the condition of model for studies in a specific contextual or existential situation, unique, independent of personal self-awareness of facts, parafacts, and the multiple dimensions in which they manifest themselves.

Heterointrusion – Condition or state of a conscin emotionally, intellectually, and energetically submissive to intrusion, or impertinent insistence made by another unconscious, energivorous, or consciously ill-intentioned consciousness.

Heterothosene – The thosene of someone else in relation to us.

Holobiography – Set of personal archives of the multidimensional evolution of a consciousness along its seriexis.

Holokarma – The reunion of the three types of consciential actions and possible reactions: egokarma, groupkarma, and polykarma, within the principles of cause and effect, or the action and reaction acting on the path of the evolution of a consciousness, either a conscin or consciex.

Holomaturity – Is the quality of integral consciential maturity of a human consciousness: biological, psychological, holosomatic, and multidimensional.

Holomemory – Integral memory: total, continuous, multimemory, or polymemory. It is the source of consciential identity which we will one day use with full lucidity, in an efficient and cosmoethical manner at all times, and without any effort. This holomemory is multiexistential, multimillennial and multigifted; our megarepository connected to our many lives and experiences.

Holosoma – Set of the vehicles of manifestation of a conscin: soma, energosoma, psychosoma, and mentalsoma; and of a consciex: psychosoma and mentalsoma.

Holosomatic homeostasis – Is the state of integral healthy harmony of the holosoma.

Holosomatology – Specialty of conscientiology applied to the study of the holosoma.

Holothosene – Is the thosenic atmosphere, or intraphysical environment fixating the set of all aggregated or consolidated thosenes; either of a conscin, or of a whole evolutionary group.

Homo sapiens serenissimus – Is a consciousness fully experiencing the condition of lucid serenism, popularly called by the abbreviation: *Serenissimus.*

Hyperacuity – Quality of maximum lucidity of a conscin, reached through the maximum possible recovery of their cons.

International Cosmoethical Conscientiological Community – ICCC – Is the group of inhabitants, sharing a common, daily, intraphysical life in this human, material, or terrestrial dimension in a society of conscins connected by the consciential link of conscientiology.

Ideological maxidissidence – Is the major critical moment of unappealable separation from a group institution, when the isolated part is hindering the consciential progress of the other, aiming at the development of a more advanced and libertarian idea.

Immanent energy (IE) – The primary, vibratory, essential, multiform, impersonal, diffuse, and disperse energy present in all objects or realities of the universe, omnipotently, still uncontrolled by human consciousness, and too subtle to be discovered and detected by our current technological tools.

Impactotherapy – Is an evolved therapeutic process used cosmoethically, delivering leading-edge relative truths used as a remedy, or *surgical technique,* to give a mentalsomatic shock of consciential rational heterodiscernment to misoneist neophobic conscins, haltered readers one easily finds in any audience. This therapy is directed to chronic robexis carriers, guided by anticosmoethical, autocratic, fanatical, dogmatic personalities that defend absolute, ultraorthodox, or fundamental truths, people who think they own the truth or are above good and evil.

Integrated maturity – Is the state of more evolved consciential maturity beyond biological or physical maturity, and beyond the mental or psychological maturity of a conscin; holomaturity.

Interassistantial minipiece – Is a lucid consciousness that dedicates itself to interconsciential multidimensional assistantial work, holding an overview of the evolutionary group where it is integrated, and one that is sure of its personal minor, but still productive and participative function within the maximechanism of assistance to conscins and consciexes.

Interassistantiality – Is the experience of mutual interconsciential assistance, notably based on reeducation through the use of clarification task (claritask), evolutionary intelligence, cosmoethics, polykarmality, and the cosmic principle in which "the less ill watches over the more ill".

Interconscientiology – Is the science applied to the study of the manifestations between consciousnesses, or between a consciousness and extraconsciential realities.

Interiorosis – Quality, condition, or chronic state of the *interiorot*, super-rooted and circumscribed to a small space, be it a village, neighbourhood, withdrawn suburb, or rural area, or the interior of the country, without the courage or stimulus to face the cosmovision of life beyond these narrow shrunken limits.

Intermission – Extraphysical period of a consciousness between two lives.

Intermissiology – Specialty of conscientiology that studies the period of intermission of a consciousness in evolution, understood between two of its intraphysical lives, within its existential cycle.

Intermissive Course (IC) – Is the set of disciplines composing programmes designed to encompass classes and theatical experiences, taught to consciexes of an already considerable evolutionary level of lucidity, during a period of consciential intermission (intermissiology, extraphysicology), within the cycle of their personal human lives. It is aimed at helping them achieve consciential completism (complexis) in their existential programme (proexis) for the next intraphysical life.

Intermissivist – A consciex who is a student or ex-student of a pre-resomatic Intermissive Course (IC). In the universe of conscientiology, a conscin that is self-aware of being an ex-student of an IC and of its very commitments and diverse evolutionary duties agreed to during the experiences of its intermissive prenatal period, through the direct assistance of the evolutiologist present at that particular extraphysical injunction.

Intraconsciential compass – Pointer of consciousness manifesting itself in a healthy manner, providing guidance in the cosmoethical direction of the thosenic manifestations, in order to indicate the maximum evolutionary level in favour of lived megafraternity.

Intraconsciential recycling – See *Recin.*

Intraconscientiality – Quality of the specific manifestations of a consciousness within its intimacy.

Intraconscientiology – The science applied to the study of the manifestations of a consciousness, totally based on its intimacy and core, or bosom of its intraconscientiality, when the consciousness (conscin or consciex) employs to the maximum the potential of its deepest mentalsomatic attributes and the resources of its consciential microuniverse.

Intraphysical restriction – Funneling imposed to all consciousnesses of their personal attributes when they are reborn on Earth, in a new human body.

Intraphysicality – The condition of the human intraphysical life of a consciousness, or its human existence.

Intrudability – Unhealthy, interconsciential thosenic intrusion. Equivalent expression (anachronistic): obsession.

Invexibility – Quality of a conscin's intraphysical invexis performance potential.

Invexis – The technique of existential inversion performed by a consciousness in its human or intraphysical existence (a conscin), starting before average biological maturity.

Leading-edge relative truth – *See Verpon.*

Lucid epicon – Consciential epicentre; the key conscin self-constituted as a core axis of lucidity and minicog in the multidimensional cosmoethic interassistantial maximechanism, through advanced self-conscientiality or, for example, active development of their offiex through their penta practice.

Lucid projectability – Is the paraphysiological lucid projective quality of the consciousness capable of taking the vehicles of manifestation of its holosoma out of alignment, including the ability to perform lucid projections induced by will alone.

Lucid projection – Is the projection of a consciousness beyond its physical body or soma carried out with lucidity; lucid out-of-body experience.

Materthosene – Is the mother-idea, or matrix of all development of a thesis, theory, or trial; the *leitmotiv;* the main pillar, or the predominant thosene in any specific holothosene.

Maxifraternity – Interconsciential, universalistic, more evolved condition based on the pure fraternity of the self-unforgiving consciousness (who does not forgive its own mistakes) simultaneously hetero-forgiving (a forgiver of other people's mistakes) – an inevitable goal in the evolution of all consciousnesses.

Maxiproexis – Is the wider, more advanced, more giving, maximum wholesale existential programme consciously dedicated to the welfare of a community, aiming at the accomplishment of a consciousness' clarification task (claritask), living universalism, maxifraternity, and paralawlogy, with a polykarmic evolutionary basis.

Megaeuphorization – Is the energetic state installed by the decided will of a consciousness, conscin or consciex, through the maximum exaltation of the consciential energies of its energosphere or holosoma, taken to the homeostatic apex of intimate harmony of its consciential microuniverse, with expansion of consciousness generating an aura of health, serenity, tranquility, universal fraternity, apex of plenitude, and self-disposition for interassistantial performance, all stemming from the vibrational state (VS).

Megastrongtrait – Is the major strongtrait, or predominant megatalent in the structure of a consciousness' microuniverse.

Mentalsoma – Is the mental body, or parabody of discernment of the consciousness and its most sophisticated vehicle of manifestation.

Multidimensional self-awareness – Is the condition of the mature lucidity of a conscin as regards consciential life in the evolved state of multidimensionality, reached through the power of their will (volitiology), promoting conscious projections (projectiology) in other dimensions, out of the sphere of physical manifestations (intraphysicology), that is, through lucid projectability.

Multidimensionality – Is the condition of a consciousness, be it a conscin or a consciex, living inevitably forever and acting at the same time in a conscious and an unconscious way in a number of existential dimensions.

Multiexistential self-relay – Is the act, process, or effect of a lucid consciousness relaying itself with absolute self-awareness and to maximum effect within the uninterrupted development of their evolutionary, advanced, and intentionally intertwined enterprises, in the series of pre-resomatic and post-resomatic intermissions, and its respective, intraphysical, consecutive, continued, and multimillennial lives.

Multiexistentiality – Is the quality, or the condition of a consciousness' self-awareness about experiencing continuous multiple lives throughout the millennia.

Neophilia – Is the easy adaptation of a person to new situations, things, and events.

Neothosene – Is the thosene of the human consciousness when it is manifesting through new synapses, or interneuronal connections (cortical hemispheres), generating new ideas.

Neoverpon – Is the new relative leading-edge (or vanguard) truth or veracity; the neothosene, the neoconstruct, or neoidea waiting to be discovered or unveiled through the unwavering persistence of the self-aware lucid researcher's performance.

Offiex – The offiex (extraphysical clinic, or extraphysical office) is the physical-extraphysical premises used by the veteran penta practitioner in their daily services of hetero-assistantiality. The veteran penta practitioner works here in the condition of intraphysical epicentre of this work, and this more evolved clinic becomes the extraphysical equivalent of the practitioner's human base, or home.

Orthothosene – Is the straightforward, healthy, or cosmoethical thosene, natural to consciential holomaturity; the unit of measure of practical cosmoethics, according to conscientiometry.

Orthothosenity – Is the quality, act, or effect of maintaining one's self-thosenity based on the constant predominance of orthothosenes, those straightforward cosmoethical thosenes composing the condition of holomaturity of a consciousness, conscin or consciex, and also the unit of practical cosmoethicology.

Para – Prefix used in words to mean beyond or beside, as in parabrain. It also means extraphysical.

Parabrain – Is the extraphysical brain of the psychosoma of a consciousness either in the extraphysical state (consciex), intraphysical state (conscin), or the projected state through the psychosoma.

Paracitizen – Is a consciex of an extraphysical community.

Paraduty – Is the condition of a consciousness lucid of the commitments, norms, principles, and just, honest and correct paralaws agreed to, envisaging self-conscious development in a personal process of evolution that is intertwined with the evolution of its own evolutionary group.

Paradidactic – Is a subfield of parapedagogy dedicated to the scientific precepts capable of guiding paraeducational activity to make it more effective.

Parafact – Is the extraphysical phenomenon, occurrence, or event relative to the consciousness, be that a conscin or consciex.

Paragenetics – Is the speciality of conscientiology applied to the study and research of genetics in a composite and integral manner, encompassing the entire consciousness' holosomatic heritage, through studying its psychosoma and its mentalsoma, retrosomas from past lives (retrolives) and even the human embryo of its current life in its condition of a conscin.

Paralawology – Is the science applied to the technical and paratechnical studies, theorical research and pararesearch of the set of norms, principles, and paralaws of consciential manifestations, or just, honest, and correct thosenations, according to the cosmoethical and synchronous flow of the cosmos, from the correct use of immanent energies, in the experience and paraexperience of mega-fraternity.

Parapathology – Is the pathology of the vehicles of manifestation of the consciousness, excluding its human body or soma. It is a speciality of conscientiology.

Parapedagogue – Is the teacher, educator, preceptor, instructor, or trainer using the resources and techniques of conscientiology, or more specifically of parapedagogy.

Paraperceptiology – Is the speciality of conscientiology applied to the studies and research of the consciousness′ paraperceptions, or of its parapsychism, beyond the perceptions of the human body (soma), arising phenomena and evolutionary consequences.

Paraperception – *See parapsychism.*

Paraphenomenon – Is an occurrence of a parapsychic, energetic, holosomatic, or even projective nature.

Paraphysiology – Is the physiology of the vehicles of manifestation of the consciousness, excluding the human body, or soma. It is a speciality of conscientiology.

Paraprovenance – Is the extraphysical, original, personal home base from where each intraphysical consciousness (conscin) comes, prior to rebirth, or resoma, when they were in the pre-resomatic period in the condition of extraphysical consciousness (consciex).

Parapsychic signals – Self-awareness about the existence, identification, record, and use of one′s personal animic energetic parapsychic signals, or the transcendent indisputable perception of the presence of consciexes, or of extraphysical occurrences, parafacts, and paraphenomena happening around the paraperceptive person in the normal waking state, or when the conscin is projected with lucidity beyond the physical body.

Parapsychism – Is the condition of the human consciousness (conscin) capable of experiencing paraperceptions that extend beyond the senses of the physical body (soma).

Paratroposphere – Is the tropospheric extraphysical dimension, layer surrounding the Earth's surface.

Pathothosene – Is the pathological thosene, mental peccadillo specific to consciential dementia, or to a consciousness intoxicated by anticosmoethics.

Penta – Personal energetic task performed daily and multidimensionally, always with the assistance of helpers, long-term, or for the remainder of the intraphysical life of the respective penta practitioner.

Penta practitioner – Is a conscin performing their daily personal energetic task.

Personal Code of Cosmoethics (PCC) – Is the systematic compilation, or set of norms of correctness, orthothosenity and polykarmic self-behaviour of the highest moral degree, created and followed by the more lucid consciousness, in any existential dimension.

Personal Evolutionary Record (PER) – Is the extraphysical register, ordered set of information and more intimate and detailed characteristics of essential thosenic manifestations relative to one's self-experiences, or to the microuniverse of a consciential principle, always updated or filled in paratechnologically, under the responsibility of an evolutiologist, or the extraphysical evolutionary advisor of one's groupkarma.

Personal Multiexistential Cycle (PMC) – Is the time interval during which the sequence of successive, regularly recurring events or phenomena of the system, or condition of continuous, multisomatic and multimillennial alternation gets completed, at the current average level of consciential evolution, from the period of intraphysical rebirth (pre-resomatics; resoma) of a consciex in human life, with another period of post-somatic deactivation (desoma; post-desomatics), extraphysical, desoma, the return of the conscin to intermission.

Phytoenergy – Is the set of present energies irradiated by plants.

Polykarma – Is the principle of cause and effect acting in the evolution of a consciousness when centred on the sense and experience of cosmic maxifraternity, besides its egokarma and its groupkarma.

Pre-intermissiology – Is the science applied to the specific studies of the experiences of an intermissivist conscin who decides to start in their current intraphysical life to intraconscientially prepare to assist the consciexes of their closest circle in the barathrosphere, those that they left behind, when the time comes for this intermissivist conscin's second desoma, in the near future.

Pre-*serenissimus* – Is a common ordinary human intraphysical consciousness (a conscin), or an extraphysical consciousness (a consciex) still far (25%) from experiencing the condition of lucid serenism (100%) that serenology discusses, or the rational level of a *Serenissimus (Homo sapiens serenissimus),* the evolutionary model for humankind.

Precognition – Is the faculty of perception through which a consciousness manages to know specific facts which may happen in the future, including the visualisation of objects, scenes and other forms.

Principle of Disbelief – Is the fundamental and irreplaceable proposal of approach made by conscientiology as regards taking on the realities of the cosmos in general, in any given dimension. A consciousness who is a researcher should refuse to believe in any dogmatic concept in an aprioristic manner without practical evidence or reflection, examination of causes, logics, and pure personal rationalisation.

Prioritology – Is the science applied to the technical studies and research of acts or effects of the primacy of the evolutionary prioritisations of a consciousness.

Proexis – Is the evolutionary personal existential programme of a conscin, or intraphysical individual, established in the extraphysical dimension for their intraphysical life, prior to becoming restricted in manifestation, in the process of living in a human body upon rebirth in the intraphysical dimension.

Projectiology – Is the speciality of conscientiology that studies the projections of consciousness and their effects, including the projections of consciential energies to the exterior and beyond one's holosoma. It is the subject-study of the *Projectiology* treatise. It is a scientific subfield of communicology (interdimensionality).

Projection by the mentalsoma – Is the state of maximum expansion of a consciousness on a level of suprarational and suprasensory mentalisation.

Psychosoma – Is the emotional parabody of a consciousness; a conscin's objective body.

Recexis – Is the technical execution of substantial changes for the better in a human personality's intra and extraphysical life, envisaging cosmoethical evolution.

Recin – Is *intra*conscientiel *re*cycling, or cerebral renovation of human consciousness (conscin) through the creation of neosynapses, or interneuronal connections (neuroglias).

Resoma – Is *soma*tic *re*birth of a consciex who temporarily becomes a conscin again, or gets out of extraphysicality and into intraphysicality.

Retrocognition – Is the perceptual faculty through which a human being can access facts, scenes, forms, objects, events, and experiences belonging to the distant past, commonly related to holomemory.

Retrolife – Is a previous, recent, or remote human existence of a conscin in relation to their current life.

Reurbex – Extraphysical reurbanization is the change for the better of the environment of unhealthy anticosmoethically degraded extraphysical communities, sponsored by *serenissimi*, in order to sanitise the intraphysical holothosene of the areas of socins over which they exercise antievolutionary harmful influence as regards humanity.

Reurbexology – Speciality of conscientiology relating to the technical study of extraphysical reurbanizations (reurbexes).

Scale of evolution of consciousness – Hierarchy of conscientiological bands, representing the specific category, level, state, or specific period of evolutionary manifestation predominant in a consciousness.

Self-conscientiality – Quality of the level of self-knowledge of a consciousness about itself; mega-knowledge.

Self-corruption – Is the repetition of the act a person does not feel comfortable with, and which they cannot approve, whose recall, concealed in the most intimate corner of their inner self, still bothers, corrupts itself, notably from an anticosmoethical point of view, reinforcing their weaktraits, and hindering their self-evolution.

Self-discernment – Act or effect of discerning and determining the superior personal capacity of understanding situations clearly and accurately first, to later judge, distinguish, decide, and identify, separating logical from illogical, credible from improbable, homeostatic from chaotic, positive from negative, true from false, right from wrong, healthy from pathological, best from worst, ideal from absolutely mediocre, priority from dispensable, neophilic from neophobic, brand new from outdated, wheat from chaff, rational from irrational, exactness from ambiguity, wisdom from courage, prudence from imprudence, besides common sense, good intention and good will, capable of bringing greater correctness, justice, consensus, and consciential evolution to the consciousness′ decision-making and attitude.

Self-incorruptibility – Is the quality or characteristic of personal incorruptible reality of a cosmoethical and theatical conscin, based on the trinomial: self-discernment – self- motivation – self-organization, forming the basis of specific principles to live by daily, in a better or healthier manner.

Self-intrusion – Condition or state of a conscin emotionally, intellectually, and energetically predisposed to harassing themselves thosenically, with an annoying and pathological persistency, without consciential hygiene or ideational self-discipline, constituting the bases for all types of heterointrusion.

Self-thosenation – Intraconsciential elaboration exclusive to a consciousness′ act of thosenating, building different types of ideas, sentiments, and energetic manifestations, conjugated and uninterrupted, expanding their self-cognition in the contexts of endless evolution.

Self-thosene – Is the thosene of consciousness itself.

Self-unforgiver – Conscin that does not forgive him/herself in their self-discipline, as regards errors and omissions, in order to eliminate conscious self-corruptions.

Serenissimus – Commonly used short expression for *Homo sapiens serenissimus.*

Serenology – Science that studies the *Serenissimi* in general.

Seriality – Quality of a consciousness subject to seriexis.

Seriexis – Evolutionary existential seriation of a consciousness; successive existences; intraphysical rebirths in a series.

Sociex – is the extraphysical society, or society of consciexes, as considered in the studies of extraphysicology.

Socin – Is the intraphysical human society, a society of conscins, or a simulacrum of the realities happening in the sociexes of evolutionary advanced dimensions.

Soma – Human body.

Strongtrait – Strongtrait or positive component of the personality of a conscin, or of the structure of its consciential microuniverse, capable of propelling its self-aware evolution.

Superavitary omission – Is the exception conduct, be it personal or performed in a group, to be prophylactically avoided in a conscious and self-determined way, the antievolutionary or anticosmoethical action, in this case going explicitly against the normal counterflow of the still pathological socin, and against its mouldy, folkloric, mythical, sympathetic, ancestral, superstitious, and current culturally idiotic traditionalisms, even if this means facing the incomprehension of the people following the standard conduct, unwary and unconscious as they are of evolutionary intelligence (EI).

Symas – Is the sympathetic assimilation of consciential energies (CEs), made at will, or the basic act of temporarily absorbing someone else's consciential energies, reading their holosomatic, paraphysiological, and parapathological conditions, often with the spontaneous decoding of the consciousness or consciousnesses' set of thosenes.

Tachythosene – The fast flowing thosene of the tachypsychic conscin.

Tertuliarium – Venue specifically built and technically prepared to house and broadcast the daily *Tertulias* and other related claritaskal leading-edge research activities.

Theorice – Is the inseparable execution of theory and practice carried out by a conscin or a consciex.

Thosene – Is the unit of practical manifestation of the consciousness, according to conscientiology, considering the *tho*ught or idea (conception), the *sen*timent or emotion, and the (consciential) *ene*rgy all integrated and inseparable.

Thosenity – Is the quality of a consciousness' thosenes.

Thosenology – Is the speciality of conscientiology applied to the studies and research of thosenes (thoughts, sentiments and energies).

Universalism – Is the set of ideas derived from the universality of the basic laws of nature and the universe, which through the natural evolution of consciousness inevitably becomes their dominant philosophy – Cosmism.

Verbaction – Is the technique by which human experience can be guided by the interaction of theory (word, or verb) and its consequent practical manifestation (attitude, or action), in coherent daily personal behaviour.

Verpon – The leading-edge relative truth is the conformity between a neothosene, the expression of this neothosene (form), and the object of this neothosene (content), or the new reality (fact) or parareality (parafact) unmistakably there, present in the face of a conscin (self-conviction), according to the Principle of Disbelief, and obtained through conscientiological research.

Verponogeny – Is the self-disposition of a lucid intermissivist conscin to get into the appropriate interactive synchronous thosenic bands and produce, or conceive of cosmoethical leading-edge relative truths (or neoverpons).

Waking discoincidence of the psychosoma – Is the parapsychic condition of a projector conscin in which they perceive their psychosoma to be slightly out of alignment, or misaligned with the soma, during the ordinary physical waking state, generating an intensification of paraperceptions, and energetic and parapsychic phenomena.

Weaktrait – Is the weak or negative trait found in the personality of a conscin, or in the structure of their consciential microuniverse, capable of preventing their self-aware evolution.

REMISSIVE INDEX

E

F

G

H

I

Q

R

S

T

U

V

W

COGNOPOLIS, THE CITY OF KNOWLEDGE

Cognopolis (City of Knowledge) is a municipal borough in Foz do Iguaçu (state of Parana, in Brazil) created in 2009, where 24 institutions connected with conscientiology are located, maintained and developed by the work of their volunteers. Municipal law 18.887 instituted this Cognopolis, which encompasses a green area with an ecological trail, residential condominiums, and activities focused on education, culture, and research.

The Cognopolis, also known in Foz as *Bairro do Voluntariado* (the volunteers′ neighbourhood), was built based on a proposal made by Dr Waldo Vieira (1932–2015), a professor, physician, lexicographer, and dentist who also proposed the neoscience conscientiology.

Among the many existing buildings in the neighbourhood, are the Holocycle and the *Holoteca*. The Holocycle – *holo* (full set of) and *cycle* (word related to the *Encyclopaedia*) is the place of intellectual production of conscientiology. Considered an incubator of authors, it houses one of the largest *lexicotecas* (collection of dictionaries) in

Brazil, with more than 7,000 copies, an *encicloteca* (collection of encyclopaedias), and a *hemeroteca* (collection of periodicals – newspapers and magazines) with more than 600 thousand clippings.

The *Holoteca* (all collections) comprises approximately 947,000 items, of which around 107,000 are books and other writings, besides objects of many different countries and cultures. The *gibiteca* (collection of comics) is considered one of the largest in Latin America, with its 35,000 comic magazines, in 16 different languages, published in 22 countries.

Scientific events are held periodically at Cognopolis to disseminate research findings and promote debate. The writing of books and articles is highly encouraged in the City of Knowledge. Among the approximately 841 volunteers working in the institutions located in the Cognopolis, over 170 are published authors, most of themes related to conscientiology.

Open to all interested visitors, the Cognopolis is integrated in the tourist circuit of Foz do Iguaçu and also has a hotel, the *Mabu Interludium Iguassu Convention.*

Conscientiology Publisher

EDITARES – Conscientiology Publisher is one of the 24 institutions located in the Cognopolis. A scientific, educational, nonpartisan and non-profit organization, EDITARES is dedicated to the publication of conscientiology science books and magazines.

With a voluntary work model, EDITARES differentiates itself by gathering a team of unpaid editors, reviewers, and managers. The authors, all volunteers and conscientiology researchers, donate the patrimonial rights of their works, or copyright to the publisher. An editorial fund, maintained by the sale of the books, and also by spontaneous donations makes EDITARES financially self sustainable.

We invite you, the reader, to know our works.
www.editares.org.br
For more information: www.campusceaec.org

CONSCIENTIOCENTRIC INSTITUTIONS (CIS)

CIs. Conscientiocentric Institutions – CIs – are organisations whose purposes, methodologies of work, and organisational models are based on the Consciential Paradigm. The main activity of CIs is to support the evolution of consciousnesses through the clarification task guided by verpons, leading edge relative truths, which are found in the science conscientiology and its subfields.

Volunteers. Every Conscientiocentric Institution is an independent, non-profit association, that is maintained predominantly by the volunteer work of teachers, researchers, administrators, and professionals from several areas.

ICCC. The International Cosmoethical Conscientiological Community (from the Portuguese, Comunidade Conscienciologica Cosmoetica Internacional – CCCI) is comprised of the set of Conscientiocentric Institutions (which currently numbers more than 20) and the conscientiology volunteers.

AIEC | International Association for the Expansion of Conscientiology

Founded on 22.04.2005, AIEC financially supports major conscientiology projects and assists in the realisation of such projects. It also has its own projects which focus mainly on construction.

In 2014, it built the Mabu Interludium Hotel and Resort, next to the CEAEC campus. Its next project is a Cultural Mega-Centre. Designed by renowned Brazilian architect, Oscar Niemeyer, and located in Cognopolis (the suburb in which the CEAEC campus is situated), the Cultural Mega-Centre will be dedicated to the research and study of humanities, history and culture, and will host exhibitions and other events.

Website: www.worldaiec.org
Email: info@worldaiec.org

APEX | International Association of the Existential Program

Founded on 22.04.2005, APEX is a research and educational organisation dedicated to the study of one's purpose in life (or life task). In conscientiology, this is known as the Existential Programme. APEX studies the life task on both an individual and collective level, as sometimes we come to this life with objectives to achieve as a group. It delivers a range of courses including the popular 4-day Existential Balance course. These are aimed at allowing students to identify their life task and evaluate their current performance in relation to it. Ideas and techniques are offered to help students take the next important steps in accomplishing their purpose in life.

Website: www.apexinternacional.org

Facebook: APEX – Associação Internacional da Programação Existencial

Email: contato@apexinternacional.org

ARACÊ | International Association for the Evolution of Consciousness

Founded on 14.04.2001, and based in Espírito Santo, Brazil, the focus of ARACE's research and educational activities is group evolution. It offers an extensive range of courses in various locations and is renowned for its three Serenariums, laboratories in which the participant spends three days alone, without access to any external communications. The purpose of this type of laboratory is to perform self-research, gain profound personal insights and contemplate one's priorities in life, with the aim of increasing the rhythm of one's personal evolution.

Website: www.arace.org

Facebook: Associação ARACÊ

Email: associacao@arace.org

ASSINVÉXIS | International Association of Existential Inversion

Founded on 22.07.2004, ASSINVEXIS is an organisation dedicated to promoting, publicising and debating all topics linked to adolescents 'sensing' they have a purpose in life and directing their efforts and resources towards realising it. In conscientiology, this is known as the Existential Inversion. Typically, an 'inverter' is aware of having made plans for this life during the previous period in between lives (the intermissive period). ASSINVEXIS assists young people (from the age of 13) to get on track with their Existential Programme and gives courses at its own campus which is being further developed in Cognopolis.

Website: www.assinvexis.org

Facebook: Assinvéxis

Email: contato@assinvexis.org

ASSIPI | International Association of Interassistantial Parapsychism

Founded on 29.12.2011, ASSIPI is a Conscientiocentric Institution specialised in the study, research, development and practical use of parapsychism, an indispensable attribute for personal evolution. With a base in Cognopolis and a presence in Portugal, ASSIPI offers a wide range of practical courses focusing on developing one's experience and control of bioenergies and parapsychism. It is well-known for its popular 3-day course called 40 Energetic Manoeuvers.

Website: www.assipi.org
Facebook: ASSIPI
Email: assipi@assipi.org

CEAEC | Centre for the Higher Studies of Conscientiology

Founded in 1995, CEAEC was the first conscientiological campus. It consists of nearly 20 laboratories dedicated to facilitating the participant's experience of a range of paranormal phenomena and insights into his or her personal evolution. It is also a research and teaching institution maintained by volunteers of diverse nationalities and professions interested in the advancement of human knowledge. CEAEC is home to the *Tertuliarium* (venue for daily tutorials on multidimensional themes); the Holocycle; the Holotheca, which house over 66,000 books and other works related to the consciousness and associated subjects; and the *Acoplamentarium* – a group laboratory that enables participants to develop their clairvoyance. CEAEC is open to individual and group visits.

Website: www.campusceaec.org
Facebook: Campus CEAEC
Email: ceaec@ceaec.org

COMUNICONS | International Association of Conscientiological Communication

Founded on 24.07.2005, The purpose of COMUNICONS is to disseminate conscientiology. It conducts and publishes interviews on leading edge topics with researchers and instructors, liaises with the media, runs a YouTube channel and maintains the Portal of Conscientiology – a hub for news and details of the latest events in conscientiology.

Website: www.comunicons.org.br

Facebook: Comunicons Comunicação Conscienciológica

Email: comunicacao@comunicons.org.br

CONSCIUS | International Association of Interassistantial Conscientiometrology

Founded on 24.02.2006, the focus of CONSCIUS is to help interested individuals increase their self-knowledge – to help them understand themselves better. The organisation works with the 'Conscientiogram' a complex methodology, developed by Dr Waldo Vieira, that allows people to evaluate themselves – their personal attributes and interdimensional abilities – according to a scale of consciential evolution. CONSCIUS offers a range of practical courses designed to lead participants towards self-understanding.

Website: www.conscius.org.br

Facebook: Conscius

Email: conscius@conscius.org.br

CONSECUTIVUS | International Association of Holobiographical and Seriexological Research

Founded on 14.12.2014, CONSECUTIVUS is an organisation that specialises in the study of the series of successive lives. It conducts research and offers a range of practical educational activities aimed not only at helping participants recall past lives, but at helping them approach the topic in a rational way so they can naturally position themselves in relation to their past and better understand their present. This process can help a person understand the probable causes and connections related to certain aspects of their character, allowing them to 'fit better within themselves' and to achieve a state of self-reconciliation.

Website: www.consecutivus.org

Facebook: Consecutivus

Email: consecutivus@consecutivus.org

COSMOETHOS | International Association of Cosmoethicology

Founded on 03.10.2015, COSMOETHOS is an organisation dedicated to the research and deeper understanding of cosmoethics, or the cosmic moral, and the practical interpretation and application of such principles in everyday life. Beyond this, the COSMOETHOS team develops and widely presents numerous courses and lectures.

Website: www.cosmoethos.org.br
Facebook: Cosmoethos
Email: contato@cosmoethos.org.br

ECTOLAB | International Association of Laboratorial Research into Ectoplasm and Parasurgery

Founded on 14.07.2013, ECTOLAB specifically aims to develop independent thinking on the topics of parasurgery and ectoplasm, with a strong focus on their relationship to health. It accepts requests from the public for free parasurgery via its website. The parasurgeries are conducted weekly during an activity known as a Dynamic during which energy is donated by a physical team and is used by a non-physical team for the purpose of assisting either physical or non-physical recipients.

Website: www.ectolab.org
Facebook: Ectolab
Email: ectolab@ectolab.org

EDITARES | International Association Editares

Founded on 23.10.2004, EDITARES main goal is to clarify interested individuals on the multidimensional reality of life. This is achieved through the publication of books and other works of conscientiological content. Authors of such works are typically independent researchers wishing to disseminate their findings and/or experiences.

Website: www.editares.org.br
Facebook: Editares Editora
Email: contato@editares.org.br

ENCYCLOSSAPIENS | International Association of Conscientiological Encyclopaediology

Founded on 21.12.2013, ENCYCLOSSAPIENS is responsible for the Encyclopaedia of Conscientiology, of which there are currently 26 volumes. It supports people who wish to write and publish verbets (entries). Over 500 researchers have now contributed to the encyclopedia, which can be accessed via websites, or custom software. 26 debates are also available in English.

Website: www.encyclossapiens.org
Facebook: ENCYCLOSSAPIENS
Email: contato@encyclossapiens.org

EVOLUCIN | International Association of Conscientiology in Infancy

Founded on 29.07.2006, EVOLUCIN is an institution whose goal is to make conscientiology available and accessible to children within educational, social, family and schooling contexts. It is not uncommon for children to have parapsychic abilities. Parents wishing to help their children understand the phenomena they are experiencing from a rational, non-mystical perspective, and develop their capacities, are welcome to get in touch. Active in Brazil, EVOLUCIN offers courses.

Website: www.evolucin.org.br
Facebook: Evolucin Consciencíologia na Infância
Email: contato@evolucin.org.br

IC TENEPES | International Association of Pentaology

Founded on 11.06.2016, this organisation researches the Personal Energetic Task (Penta) in a theoretical and practical manner. Producing, as a result, courses, educational activities and technical-scientific publications that aim to improve the practice of Penta, and through this technique contribute to the consciential evolution of humanity and parahumanity.

Website: www.ictenepes.org
Facebook: IC TENEPES
Email: ictenepes@gmail.com

IIPC | International Institute of Projectiology and Conscientiology

Founded on 16.01.1988, the International Institute of Projectiology and Conscientiology (IIPC), the oldest and largest CI, is an independent educational and scientific research institution widely active throughout Brazil and noted for its excellence in courses and technical-scientific publications on projectiology and conscientiology. It offers an extensive range of basic and advanced courses, workshops and immersions for all interested individuals, giving attention to both theoretical concepts and practical applications.

Website: www.iipc.org.br

Facebook: IIPC SEDE | Foz do Iguaçu

E-mail: iipc@iipc.org.br

INTERCAMPI | International Association of Conscientiology Research Areas

Founded on 23.07.2005, INTERCAMPI is dedicated to furthering research in conscientiology. Its goal is to construct a campus in the north-east of Brazil, where it is based. It aims to build a unique infrastructure that will bring the multidimensional aspects of our reality into focus, facilitating research, self-knowledge and self-development. INTERCAMPI hosts conferences, courses, debates, free activities and congresses, in addition to being engaged in a variety of cultural projects.

Website: www.intercampi.org

Facebook: Intercampi Instituição Conscienciocêntrica

Email:intercampi@intercampi.org

INTERPARES | International Association of Interassistantial Support

Founded on 15.05.2016, this association intends to make conscientiology available to all those with very limited financial resources, who are sincerely interested in studying it. Individual attention will be given to each case and it is intended that scholarships will be formed and granted to facilitate this assistance.

Website: www.interpares.org.br

Email: interpares@interpares.org.br

JURISCONS | International Association of Paralawology

Founded on 25.04.2015, JURISCONS seeks to stimulate the experience of multidimensional mega-discernment. The study of paralawology opens up vast research areas, including those of the World State, cosmoethics, and non-violent communication, among many others. JURISCONS is active in Foz do Iguacu, Sao Paulo, and internationally.

Website: www.juriscons.org
Facebook: @ci.paradireitologia
Email: juriscons@juriscons.org

OIC | International Organization of Conscientiotherapy

Founded on 06.09.2003, OIC applies the principles of conscientiology to health. In considering health from a multidimensional, multiexistential perspective, OIC serves to re-educate and re-define the current global view of health. It has a team of fully qualified and practising psychiatrists, psychologists, and medical doctors who, in addition to carrying out research, providing counselling to people in need, analysing and considering their issues within the consciential paradigm.

Website: www.oic.org.br
Facebook: OIC – Organização Internacional de Consciencioterapia
Email: aco@oic.org.br

ORTHOCOGNITIVUS – International Association for the Implantation of the Cognopolis of SC

Founded on 18.05.2018, ORTHOCOGNITIVUS aims planning, enabling, and consolidating initiatives that allow the implantation and support of a Cognopolis in greater Florianopolis, Santa Catarina, Brazil, with the purpose of agglutinating intermissivists and working towards the prophylaxis of proexological deviationism, interacting with the interassistantial maximechanism in favour of planetary extraphysical reurbanization.

Website: www.orthocognitivus.org
Facebook: fb.com/Orthocognitivus
Email: contato@orthocognitivus.org

REAPRENDENTIA | International Association of Parapedagogy and Conscientia Reeducation

Founded on 21.10.2007, REAPRENDENTIA specializes in conscientiological education. It develops and conducts training to enable interested individuals to become teachers of conscientiology, and also conducts research related to conscientiology and parapedagogy. REAPRENDENTIA is well-known for a course entitled PAE (Programme for the Acceleration of Erudition), which is aimed at developing one's personal erudition (knowledge acquired by study, research, and learning). In addition to hosting activities in Brazil, the organisation has a presence in Fort Lauderdale, USA.

Website: www.reaprendentia.org
Facebook: Reaprendentia Foz Do Iguaçu
E-mail: contato@reaprendentia.org

UNICIN | Union of International Conscientiocentric Institutions

Founded on 22.01.2005, UNICIN has administrative oversight of the ICCC. It provides support, guidance and orientation to new organisations, liaises with the individual organisations and mediates at a supra-institutional level.

Website: www.unicin.org
E-mail: unicin@unicin.org

UNIESCON | International Union of Conscientiology Writers

Founded on 23.11.2008, UNIESCON is a Conscientiocentric Institution comprised of authors of conscientiological books. It facilitates exchange among writers and promotes the qualification of leading edge relative truths (known in conscientiology as verpons) and masterpieces. It offers writing workshops, and provides mentors and other support to writers.

Website: www.uniescon.org.br
Facebook: Uniescon – União Internacional de Escritores da Conscienciologia
E-mail: uniesconccci@gmail.com

For general information on conscientiology, Cognopolis, post-materialistic sciences, links to free resources, and to register your interest in activities visit: www.isicons.org

For information regarding assistantial projects, opportunities, and initiatives in Africa, and globally, visit: http://www.interconsglobal.org

PUBLICATIONS BY EDITARES

Authors	Titles (in English)
Alessandra Nascimento e Felix Wong (Orgs.)	CONSCIENTIOLOGY IS NEWS: PROJECTIOLOGY
Cesar Machado	ANTIVICTIMIZATION
Débora Klippel	THE LITTLE RESEARCHER MULTIDIMENSIONALITY
Eduardo Martins	CONSCIENTIAL HYGIENE
Eliana Manfroi	CONSCIENTIAL ANTIWASTAGE
Eliane Wojslaw *et. al.*	THE ENGLISH-PORTUGUESE GLOSSARY OF ESSENTIAL CONSCIENTIOLOGY TERMS
Flávio Monteiro e Pedro Marcelino	CONS: UNDERSTANDING OUR EVOLUTION
Jaime Pereira	BARBARAH VISITS A STAR
Lilian Zolet	PARAPSYCHISM IN CHILDHOOD: QUESTIONS AND ANSWERS
Mabel Teles	ZEPHYRUS – THE INTERMISSIVE PARAIDENTITY OF WALDO VIEIRA
Marcelo da Luz	WHERE DOES RELIGION END ?
Tathiana Mota	INTERMISSIVE COURSE
Waldo Vieira	700 CONSCIENTIOLOGY EXPERIMENTS CONSCIENTIOGRAM OUR EVOLUTION PENTA MANUAL PROEXIS MANUAL PROJECTIOLOGY: A PANORAMA OF EXPERIENCES OF THE CONSCIOUSNESS OUTSIDE THE HUMAN BODY PROJECTIONS OF THE CONSCIOUSNESS

Authors	Titles (in Spanish)
Alessandra Nascimento e Felix Wong (Orgs.)	CONCIENCIOLOGÍA ES NOTICIA: UNA DÉCADA DE ENTREVISTAS EN LA SUPER RADIO TUPI, TEMA - PROYECCIOLOGÍA
Ana Seno e Cristina Nievas	GLOSARIO ESPAÑOL-PORTUGUÉS DE TÉRMINOS ESENCIALES DE LA CONCIENCIOLOGÍA
Cesar Cordioli	CONCIENCIOLOGÍA
Glória Thiago	VIVIENDO EN MÚLTIPLES DIMENSIONES
Málu Balona	SÍNDROME DEL EXTRANJERO
Maximiliano Haymann	SÍNDROME DEL OSTRACISMO
Miguel Cirera	EVOLUCIÓN DE LA INTELIGENCIA PARAPSÍQUICA
Rosemary Salles	CONCIENCIA EN REVOLUCIÓN
Waldo Vieira	CONCIENCIOGRAMA NUESTRA EVOLUCIÓN MANUAL DE LA TENEPER MANUAL DE LA PROEXIS MANUAL DE LA PAREJA EVOLUTIVA PROYECCIONES DE LA CONCIENCIA

Authors	Titles (in German)
Jayme Pereira	BARBARAH FLIEGT ZUM STERN

Authors	Titles (in Romanian)
Waldo Vieira	MANUAL DE PENTA

Authors	Titles (in Portuguese)
Adriana Kauati	SÍNDROME DO IMPOSTOR
Adriana Lopes	SENSOS EVOLUTIVOS E CONTRASSENSOS REGRESSIVOS
Alessandra Nascimento e Felix Wong (Orgs.)	CONSCIENCIOLOGIA É NOTÍCIA: PROJECIOLOGIA
Alexandre Nonato	JK E OS BASTIDORES DA CONSTRUÇÃO DE BRASÍLIA
Alexandre Nonato *et al.*	ACOPLAMENTO ENERGÉTICO INVERSÃO EXISTENCIAL
Alexandre Zaslavsky (Editor)	INTERPARADIGMAS 1 – Princípio da Descrença INTERPARADIGMAS 2 – Parapercepciologia INTERPARADIGMAS 3 – Pesquisa da Autoconsciência INTERPARADIGMAS 4 – Diálogos Interparadigmáticos INTERPARADIGMAS 5 – Precursores Interparadigmáticos INTERPARADIGMAS 6 – O Paradigma Consciencial e Outros Paradigmas de Pesquisa da Consciência INTERPARADIGMAS 7 – Transição Autoparadigmática
Aline Niemeyer	MEGAPENSENES TRIVOCABULARES DA INTERASSISTENCIALIDADE
Aline Niemeyer e Lilian Zolet	TÉCNICAS BIOENERGÉTICAS PARA CRIANÇAS
Almir Justi, Amin Lascani e Dayane Rossa	COMPETÊNCIAS PARAPSÍQUICAS
Alzemiro Rufino de Matos	VIDA: OPORTUNIDADE DE APRENDER
Alzira Gezing	INTENÇÃO
Ana Luiza Rezende *et. al.*	MANUAL DO ECP2
Ana Seno	COMUNICAÇÃO EVOLUTIVA
Ana Seno e Eliane Stédile (Orgs.)	SERENARIUM
Anália Rosário Lopes, Myriam Sanchez e Rita Sawaya	DICIONÁRIO DE TECAS DA HOLOTECOLOGIA
Antonio Fontenele	DECISÕES EVOLUTIVAS
Antonio Pitaguari e Marina Thomaz	REDAÇÃO E ESTILÍSTICA CONSCIENCIOLÓGICA
Arlindo Alcadipani	ITINERÁRIO EVOLUTIVO DE UM RECICLANTE
Bárbara Ceotto	DIÁRIO DE AUTOCURA
Beatriz Tenius e Tatiana Lopes	AUTOPESQUISA CONSCIENCIOLÓGICA
Caio Polizel (Org.)	DIRETRIZES DA AUTOGESTÃO EXISTENCIAL
Cesar Cordioli	CALEPINO CONSCIENCIOLÓGICO CONSCIENCIOLOGIA
Cesar Machado	ANTIVITIMIZAÇÃO PROATIVIDADE EVOLUTIVA

Authors	Titles (in Portuguese)
Cesar Machado e Stéfani Sabetzki	HUMANIZAÇÃO PARAPSÍQUICA NA UTI
Cirleine Couto	CONTRAPONTOS DO PARAPSIQUISMO INTELIGÊNCIA EVOLUTIVA COTIDIANA
Christovão Peres	VOLICIOTERAPIA: VONTADE APLICADA À CONSCIENCIOTERAPIA
Clara Emilie Vieira	ESCOLHAS EVOLUTIVAS
Dalva Morem	SEMPRE É TEMPO
Dayane Rossa	OPORTUNIDADE DE VIVER MEGATRAFOR
Débora Klippel	O PEQUENO PESQUISADOR: MULTIDIMENSIONALIDADE O PEQUENO PESQUISADOR: AUTOPESQUISA DE VIDAS PASSADAS
Denise Paro e Nara Oliveira (Editors)	REVISTA HOLOTECOLOGIA N. 3
Dulce Daou	AUTOCONSCIÊNCIA E MULTIDIMENSIONALIDADE VONTADE: CONSCIÊNCIA INTEIRA
Eduardo Martins	HIGIENE CONSCIENCIAL
Eliana Manfroi	ANTIDESPERDÍCIO CONSCIENCIAL
Eliane Wojslaw *et al.*	GLOSSÁRIO INGLÊS-PORTUGUÊS DE TERMOS ESSENCIAIS DA CONSCIENCIOLOGIA
Ermânia Ribeiro	DIÁRIO DE EXPERIÊNCIAS COGNOPOLITANAS
Ernani Brito, Rosemary Salles e Sandra Tornieri (Orgs.)	LIVRO DOS CREDORES GRUPOCÁRMICOS
Eucárdio de Rosso (Org.)	COSMOETICOLOGIA
Everaldo Bergonzini e Lilian Zolet	CONVIVIALIDADE SADIA
Fernando R. Sivelli e Marineide C. Gregório	AUTOEXPERIMENTOGRAFIA PROJECIOLÓGICA
Flavia Rogick	CONSCIÊNCIA CENTRADA NA ASSISTÊNCIA MUDAR OU MUDAR
Flávio Amado (Org.)	TEÁTICAS DA TENEPES
Flávio Buononato	ANUÁRIO DA CONSCIENCIOLOGIA 2012 ANUÁRIO DA CONSCIENCIOLOGIA 2013 ANUÁRIO DA CONSCIENCIOLOGIA 2014 FATOS E PARAFATOS DA COGNÓPOLIS FOZ DO IGUAÇU
Flávio Monteiro e Pedro Marcelino	CONS: COMPREENDENDO NOSSA EVOLUÇÃO
Giuliana Costa	AUTOBIOGRAFIA DE UMA PERSONALIDADE CONSECUTIVA
Graça Razera	HIPERATIVIDADE EFICAZ
Guilherme Kunz	MANUAL DO MATERPENSENE
Ione Rosa	ACERTOS GRUPOCÁRMICOS
Isabel Manfroi	O EMPREENDEDORISMO REURBANIZADOR DE HÉRCULES GALLÓ E WALDO VIEIRA
Jacqueline Nahas e Pedro Fernandes (Orgs.)	HOMO LEXICOGRAPHUS
Jayme Pereira	BÁRBARAH VAI À ESTRELA PRINCÍPIOS DO ESTADO MUNDIAL COSMOÉTICO
João Aurélio e Katia Arakaki	COGNÓPOLIS FOZ: UM LUGAR PARA SE VIVER

Authors	Titles (in Portuguese)
João Paulo Costa e Dayane Rossa	MANUAL DA CONSCIN-COBAIA
João Ricardo Schneider	HISTÓRIA DO PARAPSIQUISMO
Jovilde Montagna	VIVÊNCIAS PARAPSÍQUICAS DE UMA PEDIATRA
Julieta Mendonça	MANUAL DO TEXTO DISSERTATIVO
Julio Almeida	QUALIFICAÇÃO ASSISTENCIAL QUALIFICAÇÃO AUTORAL QUALIFICAÇÕES DA CONSCIÊNCIA
Kátia Arakaki	ANTIBAGULHISMO ENERGÉTICO OTIMIZAÇÕES PRÉ-TENEPES VIAGENS INTERNACIONAIS
Kátia Arakaki (Org.)	AUTOFIEX
Lane Galdino	MANUAL DE ASSESSORIA JURÍDICA EM INSTITUIÇÕES CONSCIENCIOCÊNTRICAS (ICs)
Laura Sánchez	LASTANOSA: MEMÓRIA E HISTÓRIA DO INTELECTUAL E HOLOTECÁRIO DO SÉCULO XVII
Lilian Zolet	PARAPSIQUISMO NA INFÂNCIA
Lilian Zolet e Flavio Buononato	MANUAL DO ACOPLAMENTARIUM
Lilian Zolet e Guilherme Kunz (Orgs.)	ACOPLAMENTARIUM: PRIMEIRA DÉCADA
Lourdes Pinheiro e Felipe Araújo	DICIONÁRIO DE VERBOS CONJUGADOS DA LÍNGUA PORTUGUESA
Luciana Lavôr (Org.)	I NOITE DE GALA MNEMÔNICA – HISTÓRIA ILUSTRADA
Luciano Vicenzi	CORAGEM PARA EVOLUIR
Lucy Lufti	VOLTEI PARA CONTAR
Luiz Bonassi	PARADOXOS
Mabel Teles	PROFILAXIA DAS MANIPULAÇÕES CONSCIENCIAIS ZÉFIRO – A PARAIDENTIDADE INTERMISSIVA DE WALDO VIEIRA
Málu Balona	AUTOCURA ATRAVÉS DA RECONCILIAÇÃO SÍNDROME DO ESTRANGEIRO
Marcelo da Luz	ONDE A RELIGIÃO TERMINA ?
Maria Helena Lagrota	MINHAS QUATRO ESTAÇÕES
Maria Tereza Bolzan	ENERGIAS
Maria Thereza Lacerda	A PEDRA DO CAMINHO
Marilza de Andrade	PROJEÇÕES ASSISTENCIAIS
Marina Thomaz e Antonio Pitaguari (Orgs.)	TENEPES: ASSISTÊNCIA INTERDIMENSIONAL LÚCIDA
Marlene Koller	DA CONSCIÊNCIA REBELDE À HOLOCONVIVIALIDADE PACÍFICA
Marta Ramiro	MANUAL DA TÉCNICA DA RECÉXIS
Maximiliano Haymann	PRESCRIÇÕES PARA O AUTODESASSÉDIO SÍNDROME DO OSTRACISMO
Miriam Kunz	ANTROPOZOOCONVIVIOLOGIA
Moacir Gonçalves e Rosemary Salles	DINÂMICAS PARAPSÍQUICAS
Neida Cardozo	SÍNDROME DA DISPERSÃO CONSCIENCIAL
Osmar Ramos Filho	CRISTO ESPERA POR TI (Edição comentada)
Oswaldo Vernet	DESCRENCIOGRAMA: FUNDAMENTAÇÃO E TEÁTICA

Authors	Titles (in Portuguese)
Paulo Mello	EVOLUTIVIDADE PLANEJADA
Pedro Fernandes	SERIEXOLOGIA: EVOLUÇÃO MULTIEXISTENCIAL LÚCIDA
Phelipe Mansur	EMPREENDEDORISMO EVOLUTIVO
Reinalda Fritzen	CAMINHOS DA AUTOSSUPERAÇÃO
Ricardo Rezende	LUCIDEZ CONSCIENCIAL VOLUNTARIADO CONSCIENCIOLÓGICO INTERASSISTENCIAL
Roberto Leimig	VIDAS DE NATURALISTA
Rodrigo Medeiros	CLARIVIDÊNCIA
Rosa Nader	AUTODESREPRESSÃO: REFLEXÕES CONSCIENCIOLÓGICAS
Rosa Nader (Org.)	MANUAL DE VERBETOGRAFIA
Roseli Oliveira	DICIONÁRIO DE EUFEMISMOS DA LÍNGUA PORTUGUESA
Rosemary Salles	CONSCIÊNCIA EM REVOLUÇÃO
Sandra Tornieri	MAPEAMENTO DA SINALÉTICA ENERGÉTICA PARAPSÍQUICA
Selma Prata	O CÉREBRO ENVELHECE E O PARACÉREBRO ENRIQUECE
Silda Dries	TEORIA E PRÁTICA DA EXPERIÊNCIA FORA DO CORPO
Sissi Prado Lopes (Org.)	CONSCIENTIOTHERAPIA
Tathiana Mota	CURSO INTERMISSIVO
Tatiana Lopes	DESENVOLVIMENTO DA PROJETABILIDADE LÚCIDA
Tony Musskopf	AUTENTICIDADE CONSCIENCIAL
Vera Hoffmann	SEM MEDO DA MORTE
Vera Tanuri	PERDÃO: OPÇÃO COSMOÉTICA DE SEGUIR EM FRENTE
Victor Strate Bolfe	ESTADO VIBRACIONAL: VIVÊNCIA E AUTOQUALIFICAÇÃO
Wagner Alegretti	RETROCOGNIÇÕES
Wagner Strachicini	CONSCIÊNCIA ANTIDOGMÁTICA
Waldo Vieira	100 TESTES DA CONSCIENCIOMETRIA 200 TEÁTICAS DA CONSCIENCIOLOGIA 500 VERBETÓGRAFOS DA ENCICLOPÉDIA DA CONSCIENCIOLOGIA 700 EXPERIMENTOS DA CONSCIENCIOLOGIA A NATUREZA ENSINA CONSCIENCIOGRAMA DICIONÁRIO DE ARGUMENTOS DA CONSCIENCIOLOGIA DICIONÁRIO DE NEOLOGISMOS DA CONSCIENCIOLOGIA HOMO SAPIENS PACIFICUS HOMO SAPIENS REURBANISATUS LÉXICO DE ORTOPENSATAS MANUAL DA DUPLA EVOLUTIVA MANUAL DA PROÉXIS MANUAL DA TENEPES MANUAL DE REDAÇÃO DA CONSCIENCIOLOGIA MANUAL DOS MEGAPENSENES TRIVOCABULARES MÁXIMAS DA CONSCIENCIOLOGIA MINIDEFINIÇÕES DA CONSCIENCIOLOGIA NOSSA EVOLUÇÃO O QUE É A CONSCIENCIOLOGIA PROJECIOLOGIA: PANORAMA DAS EXPERIÊNCIAS DA CONSCIÊNCIA FORA DO CORPO HUMANO PROJEÇÕES DA CONSCIÊNCIA TEMAS DA CONSCIENCIOLOGIA
Waldo Vieira *et al.*	ENCICLOPÉDIA DA CONSCIENCIOLOGIA

CESAR CORDIOLI

Born on October 6, 1972, in Florianópolis, Santa Catarina, Brazil, Cesar Cordioli is an entrepreneur and attorney. Graduated in Business Administration at ESAG / UDESC, Mechanical Production Engineering at UFSC and Bachelor of Law from UNISUL. Postgraduate with a master's degree in Constitutional Law at UNISUL. Conscientiology volunteer since February 1988, he has been a Conscientiology instructor since May 1994 and penta practitioner since June 2005. He has participated in the founding of various Conscientiocentric Institutions (CIs), and he is founder of the International Institute for the Expansion of Conscientiology (AIEC), where he exerts the position of president since its creation.

1. ***Research Area:***

This book addresses topics within the area of Conscientiology.

2. ***Principle of Disbelief:***

"DO NOT BELIEVE IN ANYTHING,

not even what you're told here.

EXPERIMENT.

Have your own personal experiences."

www.ingramcontent.com/pod-product-compliance
Ingram Content Group UK Ltd.
Pitfield, Milton Keynes, MK11 3LW, UK
UKHW051912310826
14795UKWH00010B/219

9 786586 544657